Heated Waters: Tracing Environmental Intersections

Steele Andrew Darren

Published by Steele Andrew Darren, 2024.

HEATED WATERS: TRACING ENVIRONMENTAL INTERSECTIONS

First edition. March 15, 2024.

ISBN: 979-8224562053

Written by Steele Andrew Darren.

Table of Contents

Chapter 1: Introduction - Understanding Global Warming and Ocean Acidification

In recent decades, global warming and ocean acidification have gained significant attention as urgent environmental issues. The interplay between these two phenomena is crucial to understanding the complex dynamics of our planet's climate system. This chapter aims to provide a comprehensive introduction to these intertwined processes, shedding light on their causes, effects, and associated challenges.

Global warming refers to the long-term increase in the Earth's average surface temperature. It is primarily driven by the accumulation of greenhouse gases (GHGs) in the atmosphere, trapping heat from the sun and leading to increased thermal energy in the Earth's system. The primary GHG responsible for global warming is carbon dioxide (CO_2), but other gases like methane (CH_4) and nitrous oxide (N_2O) also contribute.

Human activities, particularly the burning of fossil fuels such as coal, oil, and natural gas, have drastically increased the concentration of CO_2 in the atmosphere since the industrial revolution. Deforestation and land-use changes further exacerbate the issue by reducing the capacity of plants to absorb CO_2 through photosynthesis. As a result, the atmospheric concentration of CO_2 has skyrocketed, reaching levels never seen in hundreds of thousands of years.

The consequences of global warming are diverse and far-reaching. Rising temperatures have led to the melting of glaciers and polar ice caps, resulting in sea-level rise. As a consequence, coastal cities and low-lying areas are increasingly vulnerable to flooding and erosion. Moreover, climate patterns are being disrupted, leading to more frequent and intense extreme weather events like hurricanes and heatwaves. The consequences for biodiversity, food security, and human health are substantial, making global warming a pressing issue to address.

Ocean acidification is another major consequence of increased CO_2 in the atmosphere. When atmospheric CO_2 dissolves into seawater, it chemically reacts, leading to a decrease in pH and increased acidity. This is concerning because many marine organisms, including corals, shellfish, and plankton, rely on calcium carbonate to build and maintain their shells and skeletons. Acidic seawater inhibits their ability to produce calcium carbonate, ultimately threatening their survival and upsetting marine ecosystems.

These processes are intimately connected since the ocean acts as a carbon sink, absorbing a significant portion of the excess CO2 emitted into the atmosphere. While this mitigates atmospheric warming to an extent, it triggers a sequence of chemical reactions that disrupt the ocean's chemical balance.

Understanding global warming and ocean acidification is essential for addressing the environmental challenges we face as a global community. It requires interdisciplinary efforts and collaboration between scientists, policymakers, and society at large. By educating ourselves and raising awareness about these issues, we can work towards sustainable solutions, reduce GHG emissions, and preserve the health and integrity of our planet for future generations.

In the subsequent chapters of this book, we will delve deeper into the causes, mechanisms, and impacts of global warming and ocean acidification. Additionally, we will explore mitigation and adaptation strategies, emphasizing the importance of individual and collective action in combating these pressing challenges. Let us embark on this journey together, unraveling the intricacies of our changing climate and fostering a sustainable future.

1.1 Defining Global Warming

Global warming refers to the long-term increase in Earth's average surface temperature. It is a complex phenomenon that is influenced by various factors, including human activities, natural processes, and external forces.

To understand global warming, we must first define the greenhouse effect. The greenhouse effect is a natural process by which certain gases in Earth's atmosphere trap and retain heat from the sun, serving as a blanket that keeps the planet warm enough to sustain life. These greenhouse gases include carbon dioxide (CO_2), methane (CH_4), nitrous oxide (N_2O), and fluorinated gases.

However, human activities have intensified the greenhouse effect by releasing large amounts of these gases into the atmosphere. The burning of fossil fuels, such as coal, oil, and natural gas for energy production, is the primary source of greenhouse gas emissions. Deforestation, industrial processes, and agricultural practices also contribute to these emissions.

The increased concentration of greenhouse gases in the atmosphere further enhances the greenhouse effect, resulting in global warming. The average global surface temperature has risen by approximately 1 degree Celsius since the industrial revolution. This may seem like a small increase, but even minor changes in temperature can have significant impacts on Earth's climate systems.

Global warming has numerous consequences that affect the environment, ecosystems, and human societies. Rising temperatures lead to the melting of polar ice caps and glaciers, contributing to sea-level rise. This threatens coastal communities, disrupts ecosystems, and exacerbates the severity of storm surges.

Warmer temperatures also affect weather patterns. Heatwaves become more intense and prolonged, leading to increased heat-related illnesses and even deaths. Conversely, some regions may experience more frequent and severe droughts, impacting agriculture and water availability.

Climate change can disrupt ecosystems and biodiversity. Many species are experiencing changes in their habitats, migration patterns, and reproductive cycles due to altered temperatures. These disruptions can lead to species extinction and have cascading effects on the entire ecosystem.

Moreover, global warming is linked to the occurrence of extreme weather events. The frequency and intensity of hurricanes, storms, floods, and wildfires are influenced by climate change. These events not only cause enormous damage to infrastructure and economies, but also pose risks to human lives and well-being.

The consequences of global warming also extend to human health. Changes in temperature and precipitation patterns can affect the transmission of infectious diseases, such as malaria, dengue fever, and Lyme disease. Additionally, the spread of allergenic plants and pests can worsen respiratory ailments and allergies.

To mitigate the impacts of global warming, there is a need for collective action from individuals, governments, and international organizations. Efforts should focus on reducing greenhouse gas emissions by transitioning to renewable energy sources, improving energy efficiency, and implementing sustainable transportation systems. Conservation and reforestation efforts also play a crucial role in removing carbon dioxide from the atmosphere.

In conclusion, global warming is defined as the long-term increase in Earth's average surface temperature due to human activities and natural processes. It has severe repercussions for the environment, ecosystems, and human societies, including rising sea levels, extreme weather events, and threats to biodiversity and human health. To combat global warming, concerted efforts are required to reduce greenhouse gas emissions and promote sustainability at individual and global levels.

1.2 Defining Ocean Acidification

Ocean acidification refers to the ongoing decrease in the pH of Earth's oceans, resulting from the absorption of carbon dioxide (CO_2) from the atmosphere. As carbon dioxide dissolves in seawater, it undergoes a series of chemical reactions that ultimately increase the acidity of the ocean. This process has significant implications for marine ecosystems and the organisms that depend on them.

To understand the concept of ocean acidification, it is important to first grasp the notion of pH. The pH scale measures the acidity or alkalinity of a solution, with values ranging from 0 to 14. A solution with a neutral pH of 7 is considered neither acidic nor alkaline. Values below 7 indicate increasing acidity, while values above 7 indicate increasing alkalinity. The pH of seawater is currently around 8.1, meaning it is slightly alkaline.

When carbon dioxide is released into the atmosphere, whether through natural processes such as volcanic eruptions or through human activities like burning fossil fuels, a portion of that CO_2 is absorbed into the surface waters of the oceans. Once in the water, the CO_2 molecules react with water molecules and other chemical compounds, forming carbonic acid. Carbonic acid disassociates into hydrogen ions ($H+$) and bicarbonate ions (HCO_3-). The extra hydrogen ions lower the pH of the seawater, making it more acidic.

This decrease in oceanic pH has been occurring at an unprecedented rate over the past few decades, primarily due to human activities. The burning of fossil fuels, deforestation, and industrial processes have released massive amounts of carbon dioxide into the atmosphere. This excess CO_2, along with other greenhouse gases, traps more heat in the Earth's atmosphere and leads to climate change. It is estimated that since the industrial revolution, the oceans have absorbed about one-third of the CO_2 emitted from human activities, serving as a crucial buffer to climate change. However, this valuable service comes at a cost – the acidification of our oceans.

The impacts of ocean acidification are far-reaching and encompass a range of ecosystems and organisms. Increased acidity affects the ability of many species to build and maintain their skeletons and shells made of calcium carbonate, such as corals, oysters, clams, and some plankton species. These organisms rely on proper pH levels to produce their protective structures, which serve as homes or provide shelter for many other marine species. Ocean acidification impedes their ability to form and maintain these structures, thus threatening their survival.

Furthermore, the altered acidity levels in seawater can disrupt the reproductive and developmental processes of various marine organisms. Studies have shown that acidification can impair the senses and behaviors of fish, affecting their ability to navigate, find food, and reproduce. Many marine organisms, including economically important species, have complex life cycles that are vulnerable to changes in seawater chemistry. If specific developmental stages are unable to adapt to the changing chemical conditions, it could have severe effects on their populations and the overall marine food web.

Ocean acidification also has broader ecosystem-level impacts by affecting vital processes like nitrogen fixation and nutrient availability. Alterations in the chemical makeup of seawater disrupt the balance of important elements and compounds required for marine life. This can lead to cascading effects throughout the food chain, potentially affecting fisheries, marine mammals, and even humans who depend on these resources for food and livelihoods.

Addressing ocean acidification requires immediate action on global and local scales. Reducing carbon dioxide emissions is crucial to mitigate the root cause of acidification. Transitioning to alternative sources of energy, adopting sustainable practices, and protecting marine ecosystems can help mitigate the ongoing changes. Additionally, understanding the specific vulnerabilities of different organisms and ecosystems can aid in the development of targeted strategies for conservation and resilience.

In conclusion, ocean acidification is an emerging environmental phenomenon with profound implications for marine ecosystems and global climate stability. As the oceans continue to absorb excess carbon dioxide, the resulting increase in seawater acidity poses threats to marine organisms, including commercially important species and fragile ecosystems. Understanding, monitoring, and taking decisive action to mitigate the drivers of ocean acidification is essential for safeguarding our oceans and the countless species that call them home.

1.3 Exploring the Connection between Global Warming and Ocean Acidification

Global warming and ocean acidification are two closely related and interconnected issues that are having a significant impact on our planet. Both phenomena are caused by the excessive release of carbon dioxide (CO2) and other greenhouse gases into the Earth's atmosphere.

Global warming refers to the gradual increase in the average temperature of the Earth's surface due to the trapping of heat by greenhouse gases. The burning of fossil fuels such as coal, oil, and natural gas is the primary contributor to the increased levels of CO2 in the atmosphere. These emissions create a thick blanket that prevents the escape of heat from the Earth, leading to a rise in temperatures.

Simultaneously, as more CO2 is released into the atmosphere, a significant portion of it is absorbed by the world's oceans. This process is known as ocean acidification. When CO2 dissolves in seawater, it forms carbonic acid, reducing the ocean's pH value and making it more acidic. This change in the marine environment has devastating consequences for various marine organisms, particularly those that rely on calcium carbonate to build their shells and skeletons.

The link between global warming and ocean acidification is related to the increased levels of carbon dioxide in the atmosphere. As the Earth's temperature heats up, more CO2 is absorbed by the oceans, leading to a further decrease in pH levels and exacerbating ocean acidification. Similarly, the increased acidity of the oceans can also amplify global warming.

One of the most concerning effects of global warming and ocean acidification is the detrimental impact on coral reefs, one of the most biodiverse ecosystems on the planet. Coral reefs are formed by tiny marine animals called corals, which build massive calcium carbonate structures over many years. These delicate organisms are highly sensitive to changes in water temperature and acidity, and as the oceans warm and become more acidic, corals experience a process called bleaching.

Coral bleaching occurs when the symbiotic relationship between the coral animals and algae living in their tissues breaks down due to unfavorable environmental conditions. As a result, the colorful algae are expelled, leaving the coral white and vulnerable. Although corals can recover from bleaching events, frequent occurrences can be fatal, leading to the death of entire reef systems and the loss of critical habitat for marine life.

Moreover, the combination of global warming and ocean acidification has cascading effects throughout the marine food web. Many underwater ecosystems rely on a delicate balance of pH levels to support the growth of various organisms, such as phytoplankton, microorganisms, and small fish. The acidification of the oceans disrupts this equilibrium, leading to reduced reproductive success, slowed growth, and even death in some species.

Additionally, warmer oceans can affect the distribution and migration patterns of marine life. Many species are highly adapted to specific temperature ranges, and as the water heats up, they are forced to seek cooler areas or face extinction. This disruption in the natural distribution of species can have severe consequences for the biodiversity and functioning of marine ecosystems.

It is crucial to recognize the connection between global warming and ocean acidification, as addressing one without considering the other may not yield effective solutions. Efforts to reduce greenhouse gas emissions and combat global warming are vital to mitigate the impacts of ocean acidification. At the same time, active measures to protect marine ecosystems and implement sustainable fishing practices are necessary to minimize the further damage caused by these interconnected problems.

In conclusion, global warming and ocean acidification are intricately linked problems that have severe consequences for both the marine environment and human society. It is crucial to tackle these issues simultaneously, implementing measures to mitigate greenhouse gas emissions while working to protect and restore marine ecosystems. Through collective global action, we can hope to reduce the impact of global warming and ocean acidification, ensuring a sustainable future for our oceans and the life they support.

1.4 Significance of the Relationship

The significance of a relationship cannot be underestimated. Human beings are social creatures, and our relationships form the foundation of our emotional well-being and our overall satisfaction with life. Whether it is a romantic partnership, a friendship, or a familial bond, the relationships we cultivate shape our experiences and have a profound impact on our mental, emotional, and even physical health.

One of the key aspects of any relationship is the sense of connection it provides. When we have healthy, meaningful relationships in our lives, we feel seen, heard, and understood. This deep sense of connection fosters a sense of belonging and acceptance, which in turn has a positive effect on our self-esteem and overall sense of self-worth. We are social beings by nature, and when we feel connected to others, we thrive.

In addition to enhancing our sense of well-being, relationships also play a pivotal role in our growth and development. Close relationships have been found to provide a valuable platform for personal growth and self-awareness. Through interactions with others, we gain a deeper understanding of ourselves, our values, and our beliefs. Relationships serve as mirrors that reflect back to us our strengths and weaknesses, giving us an opportunity for self-reflection and personal growth. The trust and support we receive from our loved ones enable us to push our boundaries and strive for personal excellence.

Furthermore, relationships provide a sense of stability and security in our lives. Knowing that we have someone to rely on during times of stress and hardship can alleviate anxiety and provide a sense of comfort. When we face challenges, having a caring and supportive person by our side can make all the difference. Research has consistently shown that individuals with strong familial and social bonds are better equipped to handle stressful situations and tend to have better physical and mental health outcomes.

Importantly, relationships also bring joy and happiness into our lives. Sharing experiences with others, whether it is a laugh, a celebration, or a simple moment of connection, amplifies the positive emotions we feel. When we have someone to laugh with, to share our accomplishments with, and to navigate life's ups and downs alongside, life becomes more joyful and meaningful.

It is for all these reasons and many more that the significance of relationships cannot be understated. Relationships, in all their various forms, shape our experiences, influence our growth and development, provide us with stability and security, and bring us immense happiness. Nurturing and cultivating these connections is essential for our overall well-being and for leading a fulfilling and satisfying life.

Chapter 2: Historical Background

In order to fully understand the topic at hand, it is essential to delve into its historical background. This chapter will provide a comprehensive overview of the significant events and developments that have shaped and influenced the subject area. It will reveal the intricate and complex tapestry of history that sets the stage for the subsequent topics.

The journey into the historical background begins in ancient times, several thousand years ago. It was during this period that civilizations started to emerge across different parts of the world. From the great empires of Mesopotamia to the intricate dynasties of China, each region had a unique historical trajectory.

This chapter primarily focuses on Western history, where the roots of modern society can be traced back. The Greco-Roman world presents a fundamental starting point. The ancient Greeks laid the philosophical and intellectual foundation, while the Romans left a lasting impact on legal and administrative systems.

From Greece rose key figures such as Socrates, Aristotle, and Plato, who greatly influenced later generations with their perceptive insights. The birth of democracy in Athens showcased the potential for collective decision-making, albeit within a limited sphere. Meanwhile, the Romans developed a highly sophisticated legal system and governing structure that continues to shape our understanding of law and politics.

Moving ahead to the Middle Ages, Europe witnessed the collapse of the Roman Empire, leading to a fragmented political landscape and the rise of feudalism. The Catholic Church became a dominant force during this era, exerting its influence over spiritual and temporal matters. The Crusades swept through Europe, leaving a lasting impact on religious attitudes and cultural exchange.

The Renaissance ushered in a period of intellectual rebirth and reawakening. It was characterized by a renewed interest in arts, science, and philosophy. Visionaries like Leonardo da Vinci and Michelangelo revolutionized the artistic world, while scientists such as Galileo Galilei challenged age-old beliefs with their discoveries.

The chapter continues into the Enlightenment, a time when reason and rationality became the foundations for societal progress. In this era, philosophers like John Locke, Voltaire, and Immanuel Kant expounded ideas of individual liberty, religious tolerance, and separation of powers. The Enlightenment greatly influenced the political frameworks that would emerge in the following centuries.

Industrialization, with its massive impact on society, takes center stage as we progress further in time. The advent of machines, factories, and technological advancements transformed agriculture, manufacturing, and transportation systems. The repercussions extended from economic upheavals to social stratification, radically altering the dynamics of daily life.

Finally, the chapter concludes with an exploration of the two world wars that defined the 20th century. These cataclysmic events resulted in widespread devastation, significant geopolitical realignments, and ideologically charged conflicts. World War I marked the decline of the old world order, while World War II solidified the emergence of new rising powers and alliances.

By meticulously documenting centuries of historical milestones, this chapter offers a comprehensive background for understanding the subject matter. It lays the foundation for the subsequent exploration of themes, episodes, and movements that have shaped our world. By comprehending the historical underpinnings, we gain insight into the complex web of influences that define our present-day circumstances.

2.1 Historical Perspectives on Global Warming

Climate change and global warming are not recent phenomena but have a long and intricate history intertwined with human activities and societal advancements. Understanding the historical perspectives of global warming provides valuable insights into the long-term impact of human actions on Earth's climate.

One crucial historical period associated with global warming occurred during the Industrial Revolution. This era, which began in the 18th century, witnessed a rapid acceleration in technological advancements, leading to increased industrialization and human activities that significantly transformed the environment. These developments, primarily fueled by the burning of fossil fuels such as coal and oil, released copious amounts of greenhouse gases into the atmosphere, thus initiating the process of global warming.

Before the Industrial Revolution, the climate operated in a state of relative equilibrium as natural processes of greenhouse gas emission and absorption remained balanced. However, human activities such as deforestation and the burning of fossil fuels disrupted this balance, resulting in a rise in atmospheric carbon dioxide levels. This increase in greenhouse gases trapped more heat from the sun, leading to a gradual increase in global temperatures. This historical perspective highlights the pivotal role human activities played in perturbing the Earth's climate system.

While the beginnings of global warming can be traced back to the Industrial Revolution, evidence from historical sources and scientific studies suggests that significant climatic changes have occurred well before that period. For instance, the Viking colonization of Greenland during the Middle Ages attests to a warmer climate in the North Atlantic region. Greenland, known as "Vinland" by the Vikings, consisted of fertile lands suitable for farming. However, as the Earth naturally experienced variations in solar radiation and other climatic processes, a period known as the Little Ice Age replaced the warmer conditions, making Greenland uninhabitable due to ice expansion.

Examining historical climate records can reveal cycles of warming and cooling that naturally occur over thousands of years. These cycles are influenced by factors such as solar radiation, volcanic activity, and variations in Earth's orbit. By comparing these natural climate changes with the recent spike in global temperatures, scientists can ascertain the anthropogenic contribution to global warming.

However, the historical perspective on global warming is not limited to scientific data and climate records. Many indigenous cultures possess valuable indigenous knowledge on long-term environmental changes. Indigenous peoples, who have inhabited various parts of the world since time immemorial, have witnessed and adapted to climatic fluctuations over generations. Their oral traditions, cultural practices, and ecological wisdom provide unique insights into the historical changes and impacts of global warming on local ecosystems.

Understanding the historical perspectives on global warming is crucial for devising effective strategies to mitigate its effects and adapt to the changing climatic conditions. By learning from past mistakes and recognizing the long-term consequences of human activities, societies can make informed decisions about transitioning towards sustainable practices. By acknowledging the historical roots of global warming, we can collectively work towards a future where human activities are in harmony with the environment, ensuring the preservation of our planet for future generations.

2.2 Scientific Discoveries regarding Ocean Acidification

Ocean acidification is a prominent scientific discovery that has gained significant attention in recent years. This process refers to the ongoing decrease in the pH levels of the Earth's oceans. It is primarily caused by the excessive uptake of carbon dioxide (CO_2) emitted by human activities. This CO_2 reacts with seawater and forms carbonic acid, leading to the decrease in pH and subsequent acidification of the oceans.

Scientific research has identified several important aspects surrounding the issue of ocean acidification. One of the key findings is the detrimental effect it has on marine organisms, particularly those that form calcium carbonate shells or skeletons. The increased acidity of seawater makes it challenging for these species, including corals, oysters, and some types of algae, to extract the necessary carbonate ions needed for shell formation, hindering their growth and development.

Moreover, ocean acidification has significant ramifications for the entire marine food chain. As the acidity levels rise, small aquatic organisms such as plankton struggle to cope with the changes in their environment. Since these organisms are an essential food source for many marine species, their reduced availability can disrupt the entire ecosystem, leading to the decline in fish populations and other marine species.

Another significant discovery that scientists have made is the impact of ocean acidification on coral reefs. These unique ecosystems are home to a vast array of marine biodiversity, but they are highly sensitive to changes in water chemistry. Acidification exacerbates the bleaching of corals, a phenomenon characterized by the loss of algae, which provide essential nutrients and color to the reef. As a result, bleached corals become more susceptible to diseases and are less likely to recover, leading to the devastating loss of coral reefs worldwide.

The consequences of ocean acidification are not limited to marine life; they also extend to coastal communities and the global economy. Many human activities, such as fishing and tourism, heavily rely on healthy marine ecosystems. The decline in fish populations and the degradation of coral reefs can severely impact the livelihoods of coastal communities, who depend on these resources for food security and income generation. Furthermore, the loss of coral reefs can affect the tourism industry, which relies on the beauty and biodiversity of marine environments to attract visitors.

To address the threats posed by ocean acidification, scientists, policymakers, and international organizations are taking various measures. Research institutions around the world are conducting studies to better understand the consequences and develop strategies for mitigating its impact. Governments are implementing regulations to reduce CO2 emissions and limit other stressors to marine ecosystems. Additionally, initiatives such as coral reef conservation and restoration projects seek to protect and restore damaged marine ecosystems that have been affected by ocean acidification and other factors.

In conclusion, the scientific discoveries regarding ocean acidification are significant and offer crucial insights into the long-term consequences of human activities on marine ecosystems. The findings highlight the vulnerability of marine organisms, coral reefs, and coastal communities in the face of a changing ocean chemistry. Through increased awareness, research, and concerted global efforts, we can strive towards minimizing the effects of ocean acidification and preserving the health and biodiversity of our oceans for future generations.

2.3 Key Events and Milestones in the Study of Both Phenomena

In the study of both phenomena, there have been numerous key events and milestones that have shaped our understanding and knowledge of these subjects. From groundbreaking discoveries to important technological advancements, these key events have paved the way for new insights and understandings. Here, we will discuss some of the major milestones in the study of both phenomena.

Key Event 1: Discovery of Electricity and Magnetism

One of the earliest key events in the study of both electricity and magnetism was the discovery of their relationship. This relationship was first observed by the ancient Greeks, who noticed that certain naturally occurring substances (such as lodestone) had magnetic properties. However, it was not until the 16th and 17th centuries that significant progress was made in the understanding of electricity and magnetism. Notable individuals such as William Gilbert and Benjamin Franklin played pivotal roles in these discoveries.

Key Event 2: Faraday's Experimental Work

A landmark moment in the study of both electricity and magnetism came with the experimental work of Michael Faraday in the 19th century. Faraday's experiments on electromagnetic induction, conducted between 1831 and 1832, revolutionized our understanding of the relationship between electricity and magnetism. His work laid the foundation for the development of electric motors, generators, and transformers, all of which have become indispensable in modern technology.

Key Event 3: Maxwell's Equations

In the late 19th century, James Clerk Maxwell formulated the four fundamental equations that mathematically describe the behavior of electric and magnetic fields. Known as Maxwell's equations, these equations provided a unified description of electricity and magnetism. They demonstrated that electric and magnetic fields were interconnected and suggested the existence of electromagnetic waves. Maxwell's equations formed the basis for our modern understanding of electromagnetism and laid the groundwork for further advancements in the field.

Key Event 4: Quantum Mechanics and the Electromagnetic Spectrum

The early 20th century witnessed the development of quantum mechanics, a theory that revolutionized our understanding of the behavior of matter and energy at the microscopic level. Quantum mechanics provided a new framework for describing the behavior of both electricity and magnetism. It revealed that electromagnetic radiation, such as light, could be described as discrete packets of energy called photons. This insight led to the understanding of the electromagnetic spectrum, encompassing radio waves, microwaves, infrared radiation, visible light, ultraviolet radiation, X-rays, and gamma rays.

Key Event 5: Development of Solid State Electronics

In the mid-20th century, the study of electricity and magnetism saw significant advancements with the development of solid-state electronics. Bell Labs researchers John Bardeen, Walter Brattain, and William Shockley invented the transistor in 1947, which ushered in the era of modern electronics. Transistors enabled the development of smaller, more efficient, and more powerful electronic devices, paving the way for the digital revolution. This milestone formed the foundation for subsequent advancements in computer technology, telecommunications, and many other fields.

Key Event 6: Particle Accelerators and the Higgs Boson

In recent decades, the study of electricity and magnetism has intertwined with particle physics through the use of particle accelerators. Particle accelerators, such as the Large Hadron Collider (LHC), have enabled scientists to probe the fundamental structure of matter at high energies. In 2012, researchers at the LHC announced the discovery of the Higgs boson, a particle that gives mass to other elementary particles. This groundbreaking discovery confirmed important aspects of the theorized electroweak interaction and shed light on the origins of mass in the universe.

In conclusion, the study of both electricity and magnetism has encountered numerous key events and milestones throughout history. From the early observations of magnetic substances to the discovery of electromagnetic waves and the development of advanced technologies, these milestones have expanded our understanding of these phenomena. As we continue to explore these subjects, it is likely that new discoveries and milestones will shape our future understanding even further.

Chapter 3: Causes of Global Warming

In Chapter 3, we delve deep into the causes of global warming, uncovering intricate details and fascinating information that shed light on this pressing issue. It is crucial to understand these causes in order to devise effective strategies to combat global warming and its detrimental impacts on our planet.

One of the primary contributors to global warming is the increase in greenhouse gas emissions. These emissions are mainly caused by human activities, particularly the burning of fossil fuels such as coal, oil, and natural gas. As we burn these fossil fuels for energy, large quantities of carbon dioxide (CO_2), methane (CH_4), and nitrous oxide (N_2O) are released into the atmosphere, trapping heat and leading to a rise in global temperatures.

Moreover, deforestation and land-use changes also play a significant role in global warming. When forests are cut down, not only do we lose vital carbon sinks that absorb CO_2, but the decaying vegetation also releases substantial amounts of greenhouse gases into the atmosphere. Additionally, the conversion of forests into agricultural land or urban areas contributes to the decrease in carbon sequestration and exacerbates global warming.

Another key component of global warming is the growing livestock industry. Cattle, particularly cows and sheep, are significant contributors to methane emissions. Their digestive systems produce large quantities of methane gas, a potent greenhouse gas that is over 25 times more effective at trapping heat than CO_2. With the demand for meat increasing globally, the livestock industry continues to expand, intensifying its impact on global warming.

Industrial activities, including manufacturing, mining, and extraction, also contribute to global warming through the release of greenhouse gases and the emission of other potent pollutants such as fluorinated gases. These industries often prioritize productivity and profit over environmental concerns, leading to higher carbon footprints and environmental degradation.

Notably, natural processes also contribute to global warming. For instance, volcanic eruptions release substantial amounts of CO_2, although their overall impact is relatively minor compared to human-induced emissions. Similarly, the decomposition of organic matter in wetlands emits vast quantities of methane, making wetlands another crucial natural source of greenhouse gases.

It is important to mention that while natural processes have always played a role in Earth's climate system, the current level of human-induced emissions is exceeding the planet's natural capacity to absorb and mitigate them. This ongoing accumulation of greenhouse gases is gradually raising global temperatures, causing climate patterns to change and resulting in a myriad of negative environmental consequences, such as rising sea levels, extreme weather events, and species extinctions.

Understanding these causes of global warming is paramount to finding effective solutions. By reducing our dependence on fossil fuels, promoting sustainable land-use practices, implementing policies to minimize livestock emissions, and adopting cleaner industrial processes, we can begin to tackle global warming and safeguard the future of our planet. It is through our collective efforts that we can mitigate the causes and impacts of global warming, ensuring a sustainable and habitable world for future generations.

3.1 Greenhouse Gas Emissions and Their Impact

Greenhouse gas emissions play a crucial role in shaping the Earth's climate and ecosystems. They are mainly released through human activities such as burning fossil fuels, deforestation, and industrial processes. These gases trap heat in the Earth's atmosphere, resulting in global warming and climate change.

The most important greenhouse gases include carbon dioxide (CO_2), methane (CH_4), nitrous oxide (N_2O), and fluorinated gases. Among these, carbon dioxide is the primary driver of climate change, responsible for around three-quarters of greenhouse gas emissions. It is produced mainly from the combustion of fossil fuels like coal, oil, and natural gas.

The effects of greenhouse gas emissions are wide-ranging and significant. One immediate consequence is the rise in global temperatures. Over the past century, the Earth's average surface temperature has increased by about 1 degree Celsius (1.8 degrees Fahrenheit). This may seem like a small change, but it has far-reaching implications.

Rising temperatures contribute to the melting of polar ice caps and mountain glaciers. As a result, sea levels are rising at an alarming rate, threatening coastal regions and low-lying islands. Also, the increased heat causes more frequent and intense heatwaves, impacting human health and leading to heat-related illnesses and deaths.

Furthermore, climate change disrupts precipitation patterns, leading to more frequent and severe droughts in some regions and heavier rainfall and floods in others. These extreme weather events have profound impacts on agriculture, water supplies, and ecosystems. Changed rainfall patterns also affect the availability of freshwater, which is critical for human consumption and various industries.

Another consequence of greenhouse gas emissions is ocean acidification. Carbon dioxide dissolves in seawater, leading to the formation of carbonic acid. This acidification has a detrimental impact on marine organisms like coral reefs, shellfish, and plankton that rely on calcium carbonate to build their shells and skeletons. Hence, ocean acidification threatens the biodiversity and ecosystem services provided by oceans.

Greenhouse gas emissions also have social, economic, and geopolitical implications. Poor and vulnerable communities, particularly in developing countries, are more exposed to the effects of climate change. This includes increased food insecurity due to crop failures, displacement from rising sea levels or extreme weather events, and the spread of diseases in regions experiencing shifts in climatic zones.

Addressing and mitigating greenhouse gas emissions is essential to limit the severity of climate change. Transitioning to clean and renewable energy sources, such as solar and wind power, is a crucial strategy. Energy efficiency measures in industries, buildings, and transportation can also significantly reduce emissions. Additionally, protecting and restoring forests and other natural carbon sinks can help absorb CO_2 from the atmosphere.

Countries around the world need to adopt sustainable and low-carbon development strategies. This requires international cooperation and strong policies to reduce emissions, as well as adequate financing for developing nations to build climate resilience.

In conclusion, greenhouse gas emissions have a profound impact on the Earth's climate and ecosystems. They contribute to global warming, rising sea levels, extreme weather events, ocean acidification, and social and economic disruptions. Taking urgent action to reduce emissions and transition to a low-carbon economy is vital to mitigate the effects of climate change and protect the planet for future generations.

3.2 Human Activities as Primary Contributors

Human activities play a significant role in shaping the Earth's environment. From deforestation to industrialization, our actions have had profound impacts on the natural world, leading to a range of environmental issues. In this discussion, we will focus on three key areas where human activities act as primary contributors: deforestation, air pollution, and the generation of greenhouse gases.

Deforestation is the process of clearing forests and converting land for other uses like agriculture, logging, or infrastructure development. It is estimated that about 18 million acres of forest are lost each year, primarily due to human activities. This widespread destruction of forests has resulted in severe consequences for both the environment and human societies.

The loss of forests leads to a decline in biodiversity as many plant and animal species rely on forest ecosystems for their survival. Deforestation also disrupts the water cycle, as trees play a vital role in capturing and maintaining water in soil, reducing erosion and flooding risks. Moreover, deforestation contributes to climate change, as trees absorb carbon dioxide (a major greenhouse gas) during photosynthesis and help control its levels in the atmosphere.

Another prominent human activity contributing to environmental issues is air pollution. Industries, transportation, agriculture, and domestic activities generate various pollutants that are released into the atmosphere. These pollutants include particulate matter, nitrogen oxides, sulfur dioxide, and volatile organic compounds.

The release of these pollutants has numerous detrimental effects on both human health and the environment. Air pollution can lead to respiratory diseases, heart problems, and other health issues, causing millions of premature deaths globally each year. Furthermore, pollutants emitted into the atmosphere contribute to the formation of smog and acid rain, which damage ecosystems, harm soil, and can have catastrophic effects on plant and animal life.

Lastly, human activities are major contributors to the generation of greenhouse gases, primarily carbon dioxide, methane, and nitrous oxide. These gases trap heat in the Earth's atmosphere, leading to global warming and climate change. Industrial processes, fossil fuel combustion, deforestation, and agricultural practices all release significant amounts of greenhouse gases.

The consequences of rising greenhouse gas levels are alarming. They have been linked to a range of impacts, such as increased temperatures, extreme weather events, altered ecosystems, heatwaves, melting glaciers, and rising sea levels. These phenomena pose significant challenges for human societies, disrupting agriculture, water resources, and public health, among others.

In summation, human activities have undeniably become the primary contributors to several environmental issues. Deforestation, air pollution, and the generation of greenhouse gases have far-reaching consequences for both the planet and its inhabitants. Recognizing our role as active contributors is crucial in finding sustainable solutions to mitigate these adverse effects and preserve our planet for future generations.

3.3 Examining Natural Factors and Feedback Loops

In order to understand and analyze various environmental processes, it is important to examine the natural factors at play and how they contribute to feedback loops within ecosystems. Natural factors refer to the elements and conditions that exist naturally in the environment and have an impact on the functioning of ecosystems. These factors include but are not limited to climate, topography, geology, and biological systems.

One of the key natural factors that significantly affects ecosystems is the climate. Climate refers to the long-term weather patterns of a specific region, including average temperature, rainfall, and other meteorological conditions. Climate has a direct influence on the distribution of plant and animal species, as certain species are adapted to specific climatic conditions. For example, tropical rainforests are home to a wide variety of species due to the consistently warm and wet climate in these regions.

Another natural factor that shapes ecosystems is the topography of an area. Topography refers to the physical features of the land, such as elevation, slope, and landforms. The topography of an area determines the flow of water, the direction of wind, and the availability of sunlight. These factors further contribute to the distribution of different ecosystems and their biodiversity. For instance, mountains can create microclimates, causing variations in temperature and rainfall patterns on different slopes, thus supporting diverse plant and animal communities.

Geology is another natural factor that plays a role in shaping ecosystems. It refers to the study of the solid materials, such as rocks and minerals, that make up the Earth's surface. The type of rocks, their structure, and composition can influence soil properties, nutrient availability, and water retention capacity. Different types of rocks may also provide specific niche habitats for certain plants and animals. For example, limestone-rich soils support diverse plant communities, while volcanic soils can be highly fertile, thus promoting abundant vegetation growth.

Lastly, biological systems, including interactions among living organisms, are crucial natural factors that influence ecosystems. These interactions can occur within a species (intraspecific) or between different species (interspecific). Examples of intraspecific interactions include competition for resources such as food, water, and shelter, as well as cooperation for reproduction or protection against predators. Interspecific interactions include predation, parasitism, mutualism, and commensalism, among others. Such interactions not only shape the population dynamics of species but also influence the community structure and the overall functioning of ecosystems.

Furthermore, natural factors contribute to the formation of feedback loops within ecosystems. Feedback loops refer to the self-regulating mechanisms in an ecosystem that maintain a balance between various components. There are two main types of feedback loops, positive and negative. In a positive feedback loop, a change in one component of the ecosystem amplifies and perpetuates the change. For example, climate warming can lead to the melting of ice caps, which in turn reduces the Earth's albedo (reflectivity), resulting in more heat absorption and further warming.

On the other hand, a negative feedback loop acts to stabilize or reduce changes within an ecosystem. It occurs when a change in one component triggers a response that counteracts the change. For instance, increased levels of carbon dioxide in the atmosphere lead to increased plant growth through photosynthesis. The additional plant growth absorbs more carbon dioxide, ultimately reducing its concentration in the atmosphere.

Understanding these natural factors and feedback loops is essential for predicting and mitigating the impacts of environmental changes. By examining how different components interact with each other and the environment, scientists can better understand the complex dynamics of ecosystems. Consequently, this knowledge can be used to develop strategies for promoting conservation, sustainable resource management, and ecosystem restoration, aiding in the preservation of Earth's biodiversity and minimizing ecological disruptions.

Chapter 4: Consequences of Global Warming

Global warming, caused primarily by human activities such as the burning of fossil fuels and deforestation, has resulted in significant changes to our climate system. The consequences of global warming are far-reaching and have profound impacts on the environment, ecosystems, and human societies worldwide. In this chapter, we delve into the extensive and intriguing set of consequences ensuing from this phenomenon, exploring both the known and potential impacts of global warming.

1. Rising temperatures:

One of the most evident consequences of global warming is the perpetual increase in average global temperatures. Over the past century, the Earth's surface temperature has risen by approximately 1 degree Celsius. This seemingly minor change can lead to drastic alterations in the planet's climate patterns, including more frequent and intense heatwaves, widespread droughts, and heat-related health issues for humans and animals alike.

2. Melting ice and rising sea levels:

The warming of our planet has accelerated the melting of ice caps and glaciers, both in polar regions and high-altitude mountain ranges. The melting of these bodies of ice contributes to the rising sea levels around the world. Coastal communities face increased risks of flooding, erosion, and displacement due to the encroaching seawater. Furthermore, low-lying countries and small island nations are particularly vulnerable to the submerged earth, which threatens their very existence.

3. Extreme weather events:

Global warming has altered weather patterns, leading to more frequent and intense extreme weather events. Heatwaves, hurricanes, cyclones, droughts, and heavy rainfall are becoming increasingly common and severe. These events pose significant risks to human safety, infrastructure, agriculture, and ecosystems. Disrupted rainfall patterns also impact the availability of freshwater resources, exacerbating water scarcity in some regions.

4. Loss of biodiversity:

Climate change disrupts ecosystems and puts pressure on species survival. Many plants and animals are unable to adapt quickly enough to the changing climatic conditions, leading to challenges in their reproductive cycles, habitat loss, and ultimately, extinction. Coral reefs, for example, are highly susceptible to increases in ocean temperatures, causing coral bleaching and subsequently devastating impacts on marine ecosystems and the millions of people who rely on these habitats for their livelihoods.

5. Changing agricultural patterns:

Global warming deeply impacts agriculture and food production. Changing weather patterns, increased pest infestations, and water scarcity pose a threat to crop yields and quality. Traditional farming practices and cycles are becoming less predictable, which affects food security and places additional strains on already vulnerable communities, particularly in the developing world.

6. Amplified health risks:

Global warming triggers a range of health consequences for humans. More frequent and intense heatwaves can lead to heat-related illnesses and deaths, particularly among vulnerable populations such as the elderly, young children, and those with pre-existing health conditions. Additionally, changing rainfall patterns may exacerbate the incidence of waterborne diseases and alter the distribution of infectious diseases carried by insects like mosquitoes, potentially increasing their transmission rates.

7. Economic implications:

The consequences of global warming present significant economic burdens on societies. Governments and communities face increased costs in adapting infrastructure to cope with rising sea levels, protecting against extreme weather events, and implementing effective heat mitigation strategies. Disrupted ecosystems and declining agricultural productivity affect livelihoods and exacerbate poverty levels, leading to detrimental socio-economic consequences.

THE CONSEQUENCES OF global warming are undeniable, both in their scope and severity. The emissions associated with human activities continue to contribute to the acceleration of climate change, amplifying the aforementioned consequences. However, understanding these impacts provides a crucial foundation for developing mitigation and adaptation strategies to address climate change and cultivate a more sustainable future. It is imperative that societies worldwide work together in the collective pursuit of solutions to combat global warming and protect our planet for future generations.

4.1 Temperature Rise and its Implications

The issue of global temperature rise is a highly debated and widely researched topic in the field of climate change. Temperature rise refers to the increase in average temperature of the Earth's atmosphere and oceans over a certain period of time. This increase has significant implications for various aspects of our environment, ecosystems, and human societies.

One of the most evident implications of temperature rise is the accelerated melting of polar ice caps and glaciers. As temperatures rise, the ice in these regions begins to melt at a faster rate, leading to a rise in sea levels. This poses a great threat to coastal areas and low-lying islands, which face an increasing risk of flooding and even submersion. Moreover, the loss of polar ice caps greatly impacts the delicate balance of ecosystems and disrupts the habitats of various animal species, particularly those adapted to cold environments such as polar bears and penguins.

Temperature rise also affects the frequency and intensity of extreme weather events. Warmer temperatures can lead to more intense hurricanes, heatwaves, droughts, and heavy rainfall. These extreme weather events can have devastating impacts on both human lives and infrastructure. For example, the increased frequency of heatwaves can result in heat-related illnesses and deaths, especially among vulnerable populations such as the elderly and those with pre-existing health conditions. Similarly, more frequent and severe droughts can lead to crop failures, water scarcity, and food shortages, particularly in areas heavily reliant on agriculture.

Furthermore, temperature rise can cause shifts and disruptions in ecosystems and alter the distribution and behavior of various plant and animal species. Warmer temperatures can lead to the desertification of certain regions, making them uninhabitable for many species. This can disrupt ecological food chains and traditional habitats, leading to the extinction or migration of certain species. In turn, this loss of biodiversity can have cascading effects on ecosystem services, such as pollination and natural pest control, which are crucial for human well-being.

Another significant implication of temperature rise is the acidification of oceans. As the atmosphere warms, more carbon dioxide is absorbed by the oceans, resulting in a decrease in pH levels. This acidification threatens marine life, as it hampers the ability of coral reefs, shellfish, and other organisms to build their protective shells or skeletons. This not only affects the beauty and biodiversity of coral reefs, but also impacts entire ocean food chains and the livelihoods of coastal communities dependent on fishing and tourism.

Lastly, temperature rise has social and economic implications. The impact of climate change disproportionately affects developing countries and marginalized communities who have limited resources to adapt and cope with the changing conditions. Rising temperatures can exacerbate social inequalities, increase health risks, and strain already fragile infrastructure and resources. Additionally, the economic costs of adapting to and mitigating the effects of temperature rise can be substantial, potentially affecting job markets, industries, and overall economic growth.

In conclusion, temperature rise is a critical aspect of climate change that has wide-ranging and significant implications for our environment and societies. It affects polar ice caps, extreme weather events, ecosystems, oceans, and carries social and economic consequences. It is crucial that unprecedented global efforts are made to mitigate the factors driving temperature rise and adapt to its impacts in order to secure a sustainable and resilient future for generations to come.

4.2 Melting Ice Caps and Rising Sea Levels

One of the most significant consequences of global warming is the melting of ice caps and the subsequent rise in sea levels. This process, although gradual, has the potential to significantly impact coastal areas worldwide.

Ice caps, such as those found in the Arctic and Antarctica, hold enormous amounts of freshwater in the form of ice. As temperatures rise due to global warming, these ice caps begin to melt at accelerated rates. The resulting influx of freshwater into the oceans raises sea levels.

Scientists have been closely monitoring this ice melt phenomenon, and the data they have collected is alarming. Over the past few decades, the rate of ice melt has increased dramatically, resulting in a significant rise in sea levels. According to the National Oceanic and Atmospheric Administration (NOAA), global sea levels have risen by approximately 8 inches since 1880. Furthermore, satellite observations indicate that the rate of sea-level rise is accelerating, increasing at an average rate of 0.13 inches per year.

The rise in sea levels poses grave threats and challenges to coastal communities and ecosystems. As sea levels continue to rise, low-lying coastal areas are becoming increasingly vulnerable to coastal erosion, storm surges, and flooding. In fact, it is estimated that a sea-level rise of just one foot could cause more than 100 million people to be displaced from coastal regions by the end of the century.

Island nations, such as the Maldives and Tuvalu, are particularly susceptible to rising sea levels because their land elevation is low, putting their entire existence at risk. These nations could potentially be submerged entirely if nothing is done to mitigate the effects of climate change. The consequences of such a scenario would be devastating, not only in terms of millions of displaced people but also in terms of lost culture, identity, and biodiversity.

The impact of rising sea levels extends beyond human populations. Coastal ecosystems, such as marshes, mangroves, and coral reefs, serve as a buffer against storms by absorbing wave energy. However, as sea levels rise, these ecosystems are increasingly threatened. The disruption and destruction of these habitats would lead to a loss of biodiversity and expose coastal communities to additional risks.

In order to mitigate the effects of melting ice caps and rising sea levels, immediate action is essential. Efforts must focus on reducing greenhouse gas emissions to slow down the pace of global warming. This includes transitioning to renewable energy sources, improving energy efficiency, and promoting sustainable practices.

Furthermore, adaptation strategies need to be implemented to protect vulnerable coastal areas. These strategies can include building sea walls, restoring coastal habitats, and improving early warning systems for storms and flooding.

It is crucial that governments, international organizations, and individuals work together to address this global challenge. The consequences of failing to take action are severe and would result in irreparable damage to our planet, its ecosystems, and human societies. The time to act is now.

4.3 Extinction of Species and Destruction of Habitats

The extinction of species and destruction of habitats are two interconnected issues that have become a growing concern in recent years. As human activities continue to expand and encroach upon natural habitats, countless species are being pushed to the brink of extinction, with irreversible consequences for biodiversity and the balance of ecosystems.

Extinction, simply put, is the disappearance of a species from the planet. While extinction is natural and has occurred throughout Earth's history, the current rate is alarmingly high and predominantly caused by human activities. Habitat destruction, brought about by various factors such as deforestation, urbanization, and industrialization, is one of the main drivers of species extinction.

Habitats provide the necessary resources, such as food, water, and shelter, for the survival and reproduction of species. When these habitats are destroyed or altered, species face numerous challenges, including fragmentation, loss of resources, and increased vulnerability to predators and diseases. In turn, these challenges can disrupt ecological processes, such as pollination and seed dispersal, leading to further decline in species abundance and diversity.

One of the most destructive consequences of habitat destruction is the loss of primary or virgin forests. These forests play a vital role in supporting a wide array of species, including many that are still not fully known to science. The destruction of primary forests not only directly eliminates the habitat for many species, but it also releases vast amounts of stored carbon into the atmosphere, exacerbating climate change.

Habitat destruction is not limited to forests. Wetlands, grasslands, and coastal areas are also being rapidly degraded or converted for human use. Wetlands, like mangroves, act as natural buffers against extreme weather events and provide essential habitat for various aquatic species. The destruction of wetlands not only eliminates these valuable ecosystem services, but it also contributes to the loss of species that rely on these habitats.

The negative impacts of habitat destruction extend beyond the loss of individual species. Ecosystems are intricate webs, where each species plays a unique role. When species go extinct, the functions they performed, such as seed dispersal or controlling pest populations, are lost. This can result in cascading effects throughout the ecosystem, leading to further declines in other species and worsening ecological imbalances.

While habitat destruction is the primary driver of species extinction, other factors also contribute, such as climate change, pollution, overexploitation, and invasive species. Climate change, in particular, poses major challenges for species survival, as it alters temperature and weather patterns, disrupts reproductive cycles, and shifts the suitability of habitats. Pollution, whether from chemicals, plastics, or noise, can directly harm or impair the survival and reproduction of species. Overexploitation, driven by unsustainable hunting, fishing, and harvesting practices, can deplete populations to unsustainable levels. Invasive species, commonly introduced through human-aided dispersal, can outcompete native species and disrupt the ecological balance of an ecosystem.

Addressing the extinction of species and destruction of habitats requires a multi-faceted approach. Conservation efforts, such as protected areas, habitat restoration, and sustainable land-use practices, are crucial for preserving biodiversity and providing sanctuaries for threatened species. These efforts should be implemented in collaboration with local communities to ensure their long-term success.

Additionally, there is a need for global actions to mitigate climate change, reduce pollution, enforce strict regulations to prevent overexploitation, and manage invasive species. Education and awareness play a crucial role in fostering a sense of responsibility and inspiring action, from individuals to policymakers.

Preserving biodiversity and safeguarding habitats is not only an ethical imperative but also vital for human well-being. Healthy ecosystems provide numerous services, such as clean air and water, food security, and natural resources that support economies and livelihoods.

In conclusion, the extinction of species and destruction of habitats are urgent issues that require immediate attention. Human activities, particularly habitat destruction, are driving numerous species towards extinction, resulting in major ecological imbalances and potential long-term consequences. It is our responsibility to act collectively, through conservation efforts, sustainable practices, and global actions, to protect and restore habitats, ensuring the survival of species and the vital ecosystems they depend on.

Chapter 5: Understanding Ocean Acidification

Ocean acidification is an alarming global issue that is gaining increasing attention from scientists, policymakers, and environmental experts. This chapter aims to provide a detailed understanding of ocean acidification, its causes, impacts, and steps for mitigation. By delving into the intricate mechanisms at play, we can grasp the extent of this problem and its implications for marine ecosystems.

1. Acidification Process:

Ocean acidification refers to a significant decrease in seawater pH due to the uptake of excess atmospheric CO2. This occurs as the oceans act as a sink for approximately one-third of human-emitted carbon dioxide. When atmospheric CO2 dissolves in seawater, it reacts to yield carbonic acid, which subsequently releases hydrogen ions, thus acidifying the marine environment. Understanding these chemical reactions illuminates the underlying causes of ocean acidification.

2. Calcium Carbonate Saturation:

One of the most concerning consequences of ocean acidification is the reduced availability of calcium carbonate. This mineral is crucial for shell formation in many marine organisms, including corals, shellfish, and certain types of plankton. The decrease in seawater pH impairs the ability of these organisms to form their calcium carbonate structures, often leading to weakened shells, slower growth, and compromised survival rates. By examining the impacts on key species, we can assess the overarching ecological implications.

3. Biological Effects:

Ocean acidification also affects various biological processes, including metabolic functions, reproductive systems, and sensory abilities of marine organisms. Certain species, such as sea urchins and some fish, are particularly vulnerable to this phenomenon, as it can disrupt their growth, development, and behavior. Additionally, acidification-induced shifts in species interactions may lead to cascading effects throughout food webs, potentially disrupting entire ecosystems. Unraveling these intricate relationships enhances our understanding of the wide-ranging biological effects induced by ocean acidification.

4. Economic Implications:

The large-scale impacts of ocean acidification transcend ecological concerns, as they also have significant socioeconomic consequences. Affected industries, including fisheries, tourism, and coastal communities rely heavily on healthy marine ecosystems. Losses in key fisheries can lead to reduced income and food security, while degraded coral reefs can diminish tourist attractions and coastal protection. Evaluating the economic implications of ocean acidification emphasizes the urgency to mitigate its effects promptly.

5. Monitoring and Mitigation Strategies:

Understanding the intricacies of ocean acidification enhances our ability to develop effective strategies for monitoring and mitigating its impacts. Monitoring efforts encompass the collection of pH and carbonate chemistry data at various oceanic locations to evaluate temporal and spatial changes. These efforts, coupled with ecological studies, allow scientists to document trends, model future scenarios, and predict potential impacts. Furthermore, mitigation strategies may involve reducing carbon dioxide emissions, implementing ocean zoning to protect vulnerable ecosystems, advancing technological advancements to enhance carbonate availability, and promoting public awareness and policy reforms. Investigating these innovative approaches fosters the development of creative and sustainable solutions.

OCEAN ACIDIFICATION is a complex issue with far-reaching ecological, economic, and social implications. Comprehensive understanding of the acidification process, its biological effects, and economic implications is crucial in identifying potential solutions. Truly comprehending the intricacies of ocean acidification allows policymakers, scientists, and individuals to work collaboratively towards mitigating this global threat, preserving marine biodiversity, and safeguarding the well-being of future generations.

5.1 Carbon Dioxide Absorption by the Oceans

The absorption of carbon dioxide by the oceans is a fundamental process in the global carbon cycle. Carbon dioxide (CO_2) is a greenhouse gas that is primarily generated by human activities such as the burning of fossil fuels. When released into the atmosphere, CO_2 traps heat and contributes to global warming. However, around a quarter of the CO_2 emissions are absorbed by the oceans, playing a crucial role in mitigating the impact of human-induced climate change.

The process by which CO_2 is absorbed by the oceans is known as oceanic carbon uptake. This process occurs primarily at the ocean's surface, where CO_2 from the atmosphere dissolves in water. The dissolved CO_2 forms carbonic acid, leading to the ocean's natural pH level dropping and becoming more acidic. This acidification poses numerous threats to marine life, particularly those organisms that rely on carbonate minerals to form their shells and skeletons.

The rate at which the oceans absorb CO_2 is determined by a variety of factors. These include the concentration gradient between the atmosphere and the ocean, the wind speed, the temperature of the water, and the availability of carbonates in the water. Generally, higher concentrations of CO_2 in the atmosphere lead to more significant absorption rates, as the ocean acts as a natural sink for the gas.

Additionally, the ocean's capacity to absorb CO_2 is not unlimited. As the atmospheric concentration of CO_2 increases due to human activities, the rate of absorption by the oceans also increases. However, this does not imply that the ocean cannot become saturated with CO_2. In fact, some regions, such as the Eastern Pacific Ocean, have shown signs of CO_2 saturation. This saturation leads to reduced efficiency in carbon uptake and could potentially impact the overall effectiveness of the oceans as a carbon sink.

Furthermore, the absorption of CO2 by the oceans has numerous consequences for marine ecosystems. As mentioned earlier, the acidification of the water due to increased carbonic acid formation poses significant risks to marine life. For example, some species of corals, which rely on carbonate ions to build their skeletons, may struggle to survive in more acidic waters. The decline in calcium carbonate saturation could also affect other organisms, such as mollusks, echinoderms, and crustaceans, which require carbonate minerals for their shells.

Moreover, CO2 absorption by the oceans can also impact dissolved oxygen concentrations. As CO2 dissolves in water, it can react with water molecules to form carbonic acid. This reaction reduces the availability of carbonate ions, which are crucial for the formation of calcium carbonate minerals. The reduction in carbonate ions can inhibit the precipitation of calcium carbonate and ultimately lead to reduced oceanic oxygen concentrations. This has potential ramifications for organisms that rely on dissolved oxygen, including many species of fish and other marine animals.

In conclusion, the absorption of carbon dioxide by the oceans plays a vital role in mitigating the impacts of climate change. However, this process also leads to ocean acidification and has significant consequences for marine ecosystems. As human activities continue to introduce more CO2 into the atmosphere, it is crucial to monitor and understand the effects of carbon uptake by the oceans. Efforts to reduce CO2 emissions and mitigate climate change are necessary to safeguard marine life and preserve the delicate balance of our oceans.

5.2 Formation and Effects of Carbonic Acid

Carbonic acid, with the chemical formula H_2CO_3, is a weak acid formed when carbon dioxide dissolves in water. Its formation and effects play a crucial role in various natural processes and human activities.

The formation of carbonic acid primarily occurs through a reaction between carbon dioxide (CO_2) gas and water (H_2O). When CO_2 is released into the atmosphere, it readily dissolves in rainwater, rivers, and oceans due to its solubility. As the CO_2 molecules interact with water molecules, they undergo a series of chemical reactions that ultimately lead to the formation of carbonic acid.

The first step in this process involves the dissolution of CO_2 gas into the water, resulting in the formation of carbonic acid. This dissolution is driven by the equilibrium between the concentration of CO_2 in the gas phase and the concentration of dissolved CO_2 in the liquid phase. The rate of dissolution is influenced by various factors, including temperature, pressure, and the presence of other substances that might compete for CO_2 molecules.

Once carbonic acid is formed, it can undergo further reactions, including dissociation and hydration. When carbonic acid dissociates, it releases hydrogen ions (H^+) and bicarbonate ions (HCO_3^-). This dissociation reaction is reversible, as the bicarbonate ions can react with hydrogen ions to reform carbonic acid. The relative concentrations of these ions determine the pH of the solution.

The presence of carbonic acid in various natural systems has profound effects on the environment. One of the significant effects is its involvement in the carbon cycle. The carbon cycle refers to the continuous movement and exchange of carbon between the atmosphere, hydrosphere, biosphere, and geosphere. Carbonic acid facilitates the dissolution of atmospheric carbon dioxide in rainwater and its transport to rivers and oceans. This process contributes to the regulation of atmospheric carbon dioxide levels, ultimately affecting climate.

In aquatic environments, carbonic acid plays a vital role in the formation of calcium carbonate minerals. When carbonic acid dissociates, bicarbonate ions combine with calcium ions (Ca2+) to form calcium carbonate (CaCO3), which is the main component of shells, corals, and some rock formations. This process, known as calcification, forms a critical part of many marine organisms' growth and skeletal structures.

Furthermore, the presence of carbonic acid affects the acidity (pH) of water bodies. Most aquatic organisms have specific pH requirements for their survival and growth. The increase in dissolved carbon dioxide levels leading to heightened carbonic acid formation can lower the pH of water, making it more acidic. This acidification can have adverse consequences for marine life, particularly for calcifying organisms like corals and shellfish, which struggle to build and maintain their shells and skeletons in acidic conditions.

Human activities, particularly the combustion of fossil fuels and deforestation, have contributed to increased carbon dioxide emissions, leading to the enhanced formation of carbonic acid. This phenomenon, known as ocean acidification, poses significant threats to marine ecosystems and biodiversity, with potential consequences extending to larger environmental and economic impacts.

In conclusion, carbonic acid is formed through the dissolution of carbon dioxide in water and plays a crucial role in various natural processes. Its effects include modulating atmospheric carbon dioxide levels, aiding in the formation of calcium carbonate minerals, and influencing the pH of aquatic environments. However, the increased formation of carbonic acid due to human activities has resulted in ocean acidification, impacting marine ecosystems and warranting attention and conservation efforts.

5.3 Acidification's Impact on Marine Life

Marine life has been thriving in the Earth's oceans for millions of years, adapting to various changes in their environment. However, in recent decades, an alarming trend called ocean acidification has emerged, posing a significant threat to the delicate balance of marine ecosystems. Acidification refers to the increase in acid levels of the seawater, primarily caused by the absorption of excessive amounts of carbon dioxide (CO_2) emitted from human activities like burning fossil fuels and deforestation. This increasing concentration of CO_2 in the atmosphere is leading to substantial changes in the chemistry of the oceans.

To understand the impact of acidification on marine life, we must first acknowledge how marine organisms depend on calcium carbonate ($CaCO_3$), a compound found in their shells and skeletons. From microscopic plankton to larger organisms like corals, oysters, and even some fish, many rely on calcium carbonate to maintain their structure and protect themselves from predators.

As carbon dioxide dissolves in seawater, it reacts with water molecules, forming a weak acid known as carbonic acid (H_2CO_3). This process results in more hydrogen ions available in the water, lowering its pH level. These hydrogen ions then interact with carbonate ions (CO_3^{2-}), which normally combine with calcium ions (Ca^{2+}) to form calcium carbonate. As more carbonate ions bind with hydrogen ions, there are fewer remaining carbonate ions available for marine organisms to build their shells and skeletons.

The reduction in available carbonate ions has direct consequences for numerous marine species, particularly those with vulnerable life stages relying on calcium carbonate structures, such as larvae and juvenile organisms. As acidification intensifies, the formation and growth of shells and skeletons become more challenging, impeding the overall survival and reproductive success of these species. Oysters, mussels, and other bivalves, for instance, struggle to form their protective shells, resulting in weakened and underdeveloped individuals. Similarly, some species of corals cannot build their calcium carbonate frameworks efficiently, leading to the degradation of coral reefs.

Even further down the food chain, acidification affects coccolithophores and foraminifera, microscopic algae and protozoa, respectively, which play a crucial role in marine food webs. These organisms commonly serve as the primary source of food for zooplankton and small fish, and any decline in their abundance would detrimentally impact the entire marine ecosystem.

Moreover, acidification has a significant impact on marine biodiversity and overall species interactions. Certain species may be more tolerant to acidic conditions, potentially giving them a competitive advantage over others. This shift alters existing ecological dynamics, resulting in changes to predator-prey relationships, population distributions, and coral-algae symbioses. These disruptions can harm entire ecosystems and reduce biodiversity.

It is also crucial to acknowledge that acidification has indirect effects on marine life, beyond the immediate challenges of shell formation. As some species struggle to adapt to increasingly acidic conditions, their energy resources may be redirected towards combating these stressors instead of other necessary activities such as growth, reproduction, and defense against disease. This diversion of energy can weaken the overall resilience of marine organisms, making them more susceptible to predation, pathogens, or other external threats.

In conclusion, the impact of acidification on marine life is a complex and multifaceted issue. The reduction in available carbonate ions affects the growth, development, and survival of various marine species across the food chain. Moreover, the resulting disruptions in species interactions and biodiversity further accentuate the threat acidification poses to marine ecosystems. Urgent and widespread efforts are needed to mitigate carbon emissions and decrease our carbon footprint, as well as research and management strategies to help marine organisms adapt to these changing conditions. Protecting marine life from the devastating consequences of acidification is not only crucial for the health of our oceans but also for the well-being of our own planet.

Chapter 6: Ocean Acidification and Coral Reefs

In recent years, scientists have been increasingly concerned about the impacts of ocean acidification on coral reefs. Ocean acidification is a direct consequence of increased carbon dioxide (CO2) emissions into the atmosphere, primarily through human activities such as burning of fossil fuels and deforestation. This chapter will explore the mechanisms of ocean acidification, its effects on coral reefs, and the potential implications for marine biodiversity.

1. Mechanisms of Ocean Acidification:

Ocean acidification occurs when atmospheric CO2 dissolves in seawater and undergoes a series of chemical reactions. The dissolution of CO2 in water results in the formation of carbonic acid, which then releases hydrogen ions, making the seawater more acidic. This process is known as ocean acidification and has profound consequences for marine organisms that rely on the stability of seawater chemistry.

2. Effects on Coral Reefs:

Coral reefs are highly vulnerable to ocean acidification due to a process known as calcification. Corals require high levels of calcium carbonate to build their skeletons, which make up the complex structures of reefs. However, acidified seawater reduces the availability of carbonate ions, crucial for coral calcification. As a result, corals face difficulties in maintaining their skeletal structures, making them more susceptible to erosion and breakage.

Moreover, ocean acidification compromises the ability of corals to recover from physical disturbances such as storms or bleaching events. Bleaching occurs when corals expel their symbiotic algae due to stress, which leaves them vulnerable and whitened. In acidified seawater, the process of bleaching becomes more frequent and severe, and the corals struggle to recover their colorful and symbiotic algae relationships.

3. Impact on Marine Biodiversity:

Coral reefs are often called the "rainforests of the sea" due to their incredible biodiversity, supporting numerous species of fish, invertebrates, and plants. However, ocean acidification threatens this delicate ecological balance. As corals struggle to survive in increasingly acidic conditions, entire reef ecosystems are at risk of collapse.

Other marine organisms that rely on coral reefs for habitat and food supply, such as fish and crustaceans, are also affected by ocean acidification. Reduced calcification rates in shellfish, for example, impact their ability to build and maintain their protective shells. This makes them more vulnerable to predation and other environmental stressors.

Additionally, as coral reefs deteriorate, the loss of critical habitats and nurseries for numerous species disrupts the interconnectedness of marine ecosystems. This can have cascading effects throughout the food web, ultimately leading to declines in fisheries and impairing coastal economies that rely on them.

4. Adaptation and Mitigation:

While the future of coral reefs in a more acidic ocean remains uncertain, scientists and conservationists are actively searching for innovative solutions. One avenue of research is identifying coral species, or even genetic traits, that are more resilient to acidified conditions. By focusing conservation efforts on these resilient species, it may be possible to facilitate the survival and recovery of coral reefs.

At a larger scale, however, the most effective solution to ocean acidification lies in reducing carbon emissions. By cutting greenhouse gas emissions and transitioning towards cleaner energy sources, we can help mitigate the rate at which the oceans acidify. This not only benefits coral reefs but also other marine ecosystems and the overall health of our planet.

OCEAN ACIDIFICATION poses a significant threat to coral reefs and the biodiversity they sustain. As the oceans become increasingly acidic, corals face challenges in maintaining their skeletons and recovering from disturbances, while entire reef ecosystems face the risk of collapse. Mitigating the effects of ocean acidification requires concerted efforts to reduce carbon emissions and explore adaptation strategies. By taking action now, we can hope to preserve these fragile and remarkable ecosystems for future generations.

6.1 Coral Reefs - Vital Ecosystems in Jeopardy

Coral reefs are vital ecosystems that are currently in jeopardy due to a variety of factors. These diverse and intricate underwater habitats are home to a wide array of marine life and play a crucial role in supporting the overall health of our oceans. However, human activities, climate change, and pollution have all taken a toll on coral reefs, making it imperative that we take immediate action to protect and preserve them.

One of the most significant threats to coral reefs is climate change. Rising sea temperatures caused by global warming can lead to coral bleaching, a process in which the symbiotic relationship between corals and their algae breaks down. This loss of pigmentation not only affects the vibrant colors of coral reefs but also weakens the corals, making them more susceptible to disease and death. Additionally, the increase in extreme weather events, such as hurricanes and typhoons, can cause physical damage to coral reefs, further exacerbating their vulnerability.

Human activities also pose a significant threat to coral reefs. Unsustainable fishing practices, such as overfishing and destructive fishing methods like trawling, can deplete fish stocks and damage the delicate balance of the reef ecosystem. The extraction of resources, such as sand and coral for construction projects, can also wreak havoc on coral reefs, fracturing and destroying their structures. Moreover, coastal development and pollution from land-based sources, such as runoff from agriculture and untreated sewage, can introduce excess nutrients into the water, leading to harmful algal blooms that smother corals and block out sunlight.

Furthermore, the tourism industry, while conveying the beauty of coral reefs to millions of people each year, has also had a negative impact on these ecosystems. Uncontrolled snorkeling, diving, and boating activities can result in physical damage to the reefs, as well as the improper disposal of trash and chemicals from sunscreen and other personal care products. This has led to increased stress on the already fragile coral reefs, leaving scars from anchor damage and litter that impacts the overall health and vitality of the ecosystem.

Despite these numerous threats, there are efforts being made to protect and restore coral reefs. Marine protected areas (MPAs) have been created in many parts of the world to shield reefs from unsustainable fishing practices and other damaging activities. Conservation organizations and scientists are also working to develop innovative technologies and methods to rehabilitate damaged reefs, such as coral gardening and coral reef restoration techniques.

Educating local communities and tourists about the importance of coral reefs and promoting sustainable practices is also crucial for the long-term preservation of these ecosystems. Raising awareness about the destructive effects of activities like illegal fishing and littering can help change behavior and foster a sense of responsibility towards coral reef conservation. Furthermore, implementing stricter regulations and enforcing existing laws to prevent overfishing, minimize pollution, and control coastal development is essential in safeguarding these vital ecosystems.

In conclusion, coral reefs are incredibly important ecosystems that face a myriad of threats from climate change, human activities, and pollution. The degradation and destruction of coral reefs not only have devastating consequences for marine life but also impact the overall health of our oceans. It is imperative that we take immediate and decisive action to protect and preserve these fragile ecosystems through sustainable practices, conservation efforts, and raising awareness. The protection and restoration of coral reefs are not only crucial for the amazing biodiversity that they support but also for the prosperity of future generations and the health of our planet.

6.2 Coral Bleaching and Endangerment

Coral bleaching and endangerment are critical issues that are currently threatening the survival of coral reefs worldwide. These delicate underwater ecosystems, often referred to as the "rainforests of the sea," provide a habitat for a wide range of marine life and contribute significantly to the overall health of our planet's oceans. Unfortunately, coral reefs are increasingly facing severe stressors, including climate change, pollution, overfishing, and coastal development. One of the most devastating consequences of these stressors is the process of coral bleaching.

Coral bleaching occurs when coral colonies expel the colorful algae, called zooxanthellae, that live within their tissues. This algae provides the coral with essential nutrients through photosynthesis, which makes it possible for the coral to build its hard calcium carbonate skeleton. However, under stressful conditions such as increasing water temperatures or pollution, corals become physiologically stressed and expel the zooxanthellae, causing the corals to turn completely white, hence the term "coral bleaching."

Without the presence of the zooxanthellae, the coral reefs are left without their primary source of food and are extremely vulnerable. The bare, white skeletons of the corals become more susceptible to disease outbreaks and are more likely to die. Furthermore, bleached corals take a long time to recover and might never fully regain their former vibrant, healthy state. If the stressors persist for too long, the coral reefs can eventually die off completely, resulting in a loss of biodiversity and ecological functionality.

Although coral bleaching is a natural process that has been observed in the past, recent increases in its frequency and severity point to a larger underlying issue – global climate change. Rising ocean temperatures due to increased greenhouse gas emissions are one of the primary drivers of coral bleaching events. The increasing frequency and intensity of El Niño events also contribute to the problem.

In addition to climate change impacts, pollution and overfishing pose significant threats to coral reefs. Wastewater runoff from agricultural practices, coastal development, and sewage discharge introduces excessive amounts of nutrients and other harmful substances into nearshore marine environments. These pollutants can disrupt the symbiotic relationship between corals and their zooxanthellae, leading to bleaching. Overfishing, particularly the use of destructive fishing methods such as blast fishing or cyanide fishing, devastates already vulnerable coral reefs by destroying their structural integrity and depleting fish populations that maintain critical ecological balance.

Efforts to mitigate the impacts of coral bleaching and prevent further endangerment of coral reefs are crucial. Implementing effective measures to limit greenhouse gas emissions and combat climate change is paramount. This includes transitioning to renewable energy sources, reducing fossil fuel consumption, and implementing conservation initiatives to preserve marine habitats.

Additionally, reducing pollution and improving water quality through enhanced wastewater treatment systems and more stringent regulations are essential. Collaborative efforts between governments, scientists, local communities, and conservation organizations are crucial for effective coral reef management. This can involve establishing marine protected areas, promoting sustainable fishing practices, and increasing public awareness about the importance of coral reef conservation.

Overall, addressing the issue of coral bleaching and endangerment requires a multifaceted approach that involves global cooperation, policy changes, and individual choices. The urgency of saving coral reefs cannot be overstated, as their loss would have profound ecological and socio-economic implications. By taking bold actions now, we can hope to protect and preserve these remarkable and diverse underwater ecosystems for future generations.

6.3 Acidification's Role in Coral Decline

Acidification is widely recognized as one of the main factors contributing to the decline of coral reefs worldwide. It refers to the process by which the ocean becomes more acidic due to the increased levels of carbon dioxide (CO2) in the atmosphere. This CO2 is absorbed by seawater and reacts with it, forming carbonic acid. The resulting increase in acidity makes it increasingly difficult for corals and other marine organisms to build and maintain their calcium carbonate skeletons.

Corals, in particular, are highly vulnerable to acidification due to their dependence on calcium carbonate for growth and survival. Corals build their intricate structures through a process called calcification, where they extract dissolved carbonate ions ($\wedge$OCO3-) from the surrounding water and convert them into calcium carbonate ($\wedge$CaCO3). This process not only provides the structural framework for reefs but also contributes to the reefs' ability to withstand physical stressors, such as waves and storms.

However, with the increasing acidity of the ocean, corals face numerous challenges. Firstly, the decreasing availability of carbonate ions inhibits their ability to carry out calcification. The greater the acidification, the more challenging it becomes for corals to extract enough carbonate ions from the water.

Secondly, acidification impairs the dissolution of existing calcium carbonate structures. As seawater becomes more acidic, it becomes corrosive and begins to dissolve the very structures corals rely on for growth and protection. This erosion weakens the skeleton, making it more susceptible to damage from physical disturbances.

Furthermore, acidification also affects the sensitivity of corals to other stressors, such as warming waters and pollution. As pH decreases, the physiological responses of corals are altered, and their ability to tolerate other forms of stress is compromised. Therefore, acidification acts as a synergistic stressor, amplifying the detrimental effects of other factors on corals and exacerbating their decline.

The impacts of acidification on coral communities are widespread and severe. Reduced calcification rates and skeletal growth lead to the loss of reef structure and complexity, directly affecting the biodiversity and ecological function of reef ecosystems. Additionally, weakened corals are more susceptible to diseases, predation, and bleaching events, all of which further contribute to their decline.

The long-term implications of coral decline extend beyond the loss of charismatic and diverse reef ecosystems. Coral reefs provide critical habitat for countless species, support fisheries that are vital for local communities, protect coastlines from erosion and storms, and offer substantial socio-economic benefits through tourism. The loss of these valuable ecosystems due to acidification jeopardizes the ecological, economic, and cultural well-being of numerous coastal communities around the world.

Addressing acidification and its role in coral decline requires global action. Reducing and stabilizing atmospheric CO2 levels is crucial to mitigate future acidification. This can be achieved through reducing greenhouse gas emissions and transitioning to cleaner and more sustainable energy sources. Local measures, such as protecting and restoring coastal ecosystems, implementing sustainable fishing practices, and reducing pollution, can also alleviate stress on corals and promote their recovery.

In summary, acidification plays a significant role in the decline of coral reefs. By inhibiting calcification, increasing the vulnerability of corals to other stressors, and undermining the ecological function of reefs, acidification poses a serious threat to these invaluable ecosystems. Understanding and addressing acidification is paramount to safeguarding the future of coral reefs and the countless benefits they provide to both the environment and human societies.

Chapter 7: Interactions between Climate Change and Ocean Ecosystems

In this chapter, we delve into the intricate relationship between climate change and ocean ecosystems. The oceans play a crucial role in regulating Earth's climate, absorbing much of the heat and carbon dioxide emitted by human activities. However, this vital service comes at a cost to marine life as the changing climate exerts numerous impacts on ocean ecosystems. In this detailed analysis, we explore the various interactions that occur between climate change and the delicate balance of marine life.

1. Rising Sea Temperatures:

One of the most evident impacts of climate change on the ocean is the rising sea temperatures. As global temperatures increase, ocean waters warm, leading to a range of consequences. Warmer waters can disrupt the distribution and composition of marine species, affecting their behavior and reproductive cycles. Species with narrow temperature tolerances or limited ability to migrate face the greatest risk, potentially leading to their extinction. This shift in species composition can have cascading effects on entire marine food webs.

2. Ocean Acidification:

Due to the absorption of excess carbon dioxide from the atmosphere, the oceans are becoming more acidic – a phenomenon known as ocean acidification. This process can affect various marine organisms, especially those reliant on calcium carbonate for shell formation, such as coral reefs, shellfish, and microscopic plankton. Acidification inhibits their ability to build and maintain their protective structures, making them more vulnerable to predation and other stressors. Disruptions to these foundational species would have severe repercussions throughout the entire oceanic ecosystem, including declines in fish populations and reduced biodiversity.

3. Altered Ocean Circulation Patterns:

Climate change can disrupt the complex system of oceanic currents, leading to altered circulation patterns. For instance, changes in wind patterns can modify currents such as the Gulf Stream, an essential component of global ocean circulation. These altered ocean currents can profoundly impact marine life, affecting nutrient availability, migration routes, and population dynamics. Such changes in circulation patterns have been associated with shifts in the distribution and abundance of various species, including commercially important fish stocks.

4. Melting Sea Ice:

The melting of Arctic and Antarctic sea ice is perhaps one of the most visually striking impacts of climate change on the oceans. As global temperatures rise, sea ice extents decrease, affecting polar ecosystems that rely on these icy habitats. Polar bears, seals, and other ice-dependent species face shrinking habitats and reduced access to food sources, threatening their survival. Additionally, melting sea ice contributes to rising sea levels, endangering coastal ecosystems and communities worldwide.

5. Changing Ocean Productivity:

Climate change-induced alterations to ocean temperatures, nutrient availability, and circulation patterns also affect primary productivity – the generation of organic matter by photosynthetic organisms like phytoplankton. Changes in productivity can cause shifts in the abundance and distribution of marine species, including commercial fish and whales. Considering that approximately 2.6 billion people depend on seafood as a primary source of protein, changes in productivity have significant implications for human populations as well.

THE INTERACTIONS BETWEEN climate change and ocean ecosystems constitute a critical aspect of the global climate crisis. Rising sea temperatures, ocean acidification, altered circulation patterns, melting sea ice, and changing productivity levels all pose substantial challenges to marine life, biodiversity, and human livelihoods. To mitigate these impacts, urgent global efforts are required to reduce greenhouse gas emissions, protect and restore marine habitats, and promote sustainable fisheries management. Only through collective action and international cooperation can we hope to preserve the health and resilience of our precious ocean ecosystems in the face of climate change.

7.1 Changes in Ocean Circulation Patterns

The changes in ocean circulation patterns are a significant aspect of our planet's overall climate system. These intricate and dynamic patterns have a profound impact on various climatic parameters, including temperature, precipitation, and the distribution of marine life. In recent years, with the increasing concern about climate change and its consequences, scientists have been paying closer attention to these changes and how they may affect our environment.

One of the key contributors to the alterations in ocean circulation patterns is the melting of polar ice caps. As global temperatures steadily rise, the polar ice caps are melting at an accelerated rate. This excess meltwater enters the ocean, disturbing the delicate balance of saltwater and freshwater. In turn, this disturbs the ocean's density structure, altering its circulation patterns.

Another major component of ocean circulation is the movement of warm and cold ocean currents. These currents play a crucial role in distributing heat around the globe, leading to regional climate variations. However, as ocean temperatures continue to rise, the strength and direction of these currents are being affected. For instance, some studies suggest that the warming of the Arctic is weakening the Gulf Stream, a major warm current that carries heat from the tropics to the North Atlantic. If this continues, it could have far-reaching implications for the climate of Western Europe.

Moreover, changes in ocean circulation can also have significant effects on the availability of nutrients for marine life. Nutrient-rich waters often arise from deep ocean currents that bring up cold, nutrient-loaded waters to the surface. This upwelling process supports the growth of phytoplankton, which forms the base of the marine food chain. However, alterations in circulation patterns can disrupt these nutrient delivery systems, impacting the overall productivity of marine ecosystems. This can, in turn, have cascading effects on fisheries, potentially affecting the economy and food supply of communities that rely heavily on the ocean for sustenance.

Understanding and predicting these changes in ocean circulation patterns is crucial for climate modeling and predicting future climate scenarios. The Intergovernmental Panel on Climate Change (IPCC) and numerous scientific research institutions have been actively studying these changes and their potential consequences. Through the use of ocean models and data from monitoring systems such as buoys and satellites, scientists aim to better understand these complex patterns and provide vital information for policymakers and stakeholders.

In conclusion, the changes in ocean circulation patterns due to climate change are an intriguing and significant area of research. These changes have far-reaching consequences, including altering regional climates, affecting marine life and fisheries, and providing valuable insights for climate scientists. As we continue to navigate the challenges of a changing climate, it is vital to monitor and understand these changes in order to make informed decisions about the future of our planet.

7.2 Altered Marine Food Webs and Biodiversity Loss

In our ever-changing world, it is crucial to understand the intricate relationships between organisms in order to protect and conserve biodiversity. One area where these relationships are particularly important is in marine ecosystems, which are home to a vast array of interconnected organisms. However, human activities have caused significant alterations in marine food webs, leading to a loss of biodiversity and potential long-term consequences.

Marine food webs are complex networks of feeding relationships between different organisms in aquatic environments. These webs consist of multiple trophic levels, with each level representing a different position in the food chain. At the base of the food web are primary producers, such as phytoplankton and algae, which use energy from the sun to convert inorganic compounds into organic matter through photosynthesis. These primary producers serve as food sources for herbivores, which are then consumed by carnivores, creating a chain of energy transfer.

One of the main drivers of altered marine food webs is overfishing. As human demand for seafood has increased, industrial fishing has intensified, leading to the depletion of many fish populations. This disrupts the balance of the food web, as predators rely on a steady supply of prey to survive. Without sufficient prey, predator populations can decline, potentially leading to local extinctions or population collapses. This cascade effect can have far-reaching impacts on marine ecosystems, as the loss of predators can result in increased populations of herbivores, leading to overgrazing of primary producers and habitat degradation.

In addition to overfishing, other human activities such as habitat destruction and pollution contribute to biodiversity loss in marine food webs. Coastal development and the destruction of coastal habitats, such as mangroves and coral reefs, can eliminate important nursery areas and feeding grounds for many species. This reduction in habitat availability directly affects the abundance and distribution of organisms, causing changes in the structure and functioning of food webs.

Pollution, such as nutrient runoff from agriculture and urban areas, can also alter marine food webs by stimulating excessive algal growth. This leads to the phenomenon known as eutrophication, where large algal blooms deplete oxygen levels in the water, creating "dead zones" where little marine life can survive. The loss of oxygen and subsequent death of organisms disrupts the normal functioning of the food web, as it affects the entire trophic structure.

The consequences of altered marine food webs and biodiversity loss are significant and wide-ranging. The loss of predator species can trigger an increase in the abundance of lower trophic level organisms, which in turn can impact the availability of resources for other species. This domino effect can ultimately disrupt the stability of the entire ecosystem, leading to a decline in overall biodiversity.

Furthermore, altered food webs can have direct implications for human populations that depend on marine resources for food and livelihoods. Local communities that rely on fishing as their main source of income can suffer economically as fish populations decline. Additionally, the loss of marine biodiversity can result in a decrease in ecosystem services, such as coastal protection and nutrient cycling, which are essential for human well-being.

Addressing the issue of altered marine food webs and biodiversity loss requires a multifaceted approach. Implementing sustainable fishing practices, such as establishing marine protected areas and promoting ecosystem-based management, can help mitigate the impacts of overfishing and protect critical habitats. Additionally, reducing pollution and addressing climate change can contribute to the preservation and restoration of marine ecosystems.

In conclusion, altered marine food webs and biodiversity loss pose significant challenges to the health and stability of marine ecosystems. The depletion of fish populations, destruction of habitats, and pollution all contribute to this problem, with consequences that extend beyond the natural environment. By implementing sustainable practices and taking steps to protect and restore marine ecosystems, we can work towards the conservation of biodiversity and ensure the long-term health of our oceans.

7.3 Effect of Ocean Acidification on Shellfish and Plankton

Ocean acidification, a consequence of increased carbon dioxide (CO2) emissions, can have devastating effects on shellfish and plankton in marine ecosystems. Shellfish, such as oysters, clams, and mussels, rely on calcium carbonate to build their protective shells or skeletons. Plankton, including tiny organisms like algae and certain types of bacteria, are crucial for the survival of marine ecosystems as they serve as the base of the food chain.

The process of ocean acidification begins when CO2 from the atmosphere dissolves into seawater. Once dissolved, CO2 reacts with water molecules, forming carbonic acid. This reaction increases the concentration of hydrogen ions in the water, reducing the pH level and making it more acidic. The decrease in pH is problematic for shellfish and plankton as it hinders their ability to form and maintain their calcium carbonate structures.

For shellfish, a decrease in seawater pH poses a serious challenge. CaCO3 becomes less soluble in an acidic environment, making it difficult for shellfish to extract the necessary calcium ions needed for shell formation. As a result, shell growth is slowed, weakened, or even completely stalled. Weaker shells make shellfish vulnerable to predation, disease, and environmental stressors such as wave action and sedimentation.

In addition, ocean acidification affects the ability of shellfish to reproduce and grow. Studies have shown that oysters and other bivalves experience reduced reproductive success in more acidic waters. Female oysters produce fewer and smaller eggs, while the larvae that do hatch are more likely to have developmental deformities. These disruptions in reproductive cycles can have long-term impacts on shellfish populations, reducing their ability to recover from declines caused by fishing pressure or other stressors.

Plankton, the microscopic organisms that float near the ocean's surface, form the foundation of the marine food web. These tiny organisms are not only consumed by larger organisms but also produce a significant amount of the oxygen we breathe. Ocean acidification can have detrimental effects on plankton cells, threatening the stability of marine ecosystems.

While some studies suggest that certain species of plankton may benefit from increased CO2 levels and atmospheric warming, others show negative impacts on growth, reproduction, and overall fitness. Changes in ocean chemistry can directly damage plankton cells and reduce the availability of essential nutrients. For example, decreased carbonate availability can limit the ability of calcifying plankton to form its shells or exoskeletons.

The negative effects of ocean acidification on plankton have implications for the entire food chain. When plankton populations decline or are compromised, the organisms that feed on them, such as fish, marine mammals, and even seabirds, face the risk of reduced food availability. Such cascading effects can disrupt entire ecosystems, leading to declines in biodiversity and productivity.

In conclusion, ocean acidification poses significant threats to shellfish and plankton in marine ecosystems. The decreased pH and increased acidity disrupt the ability of shellfish to form their protective shells, making them more vulnerable to predation and environmental stress. Plankton, as the base of the food chain, also suffer from reduced growth, reproduction, and nutrient availability. These impacts can have far-reaching consequences for marine ecosystems and the services they provide to humans, highlighting the urgent need to reduce CO2 emissions and mitigate ocean acidification.

Chapter 8: Feedback Loops and Tipping Points

In this chapter, we will delve into the concept of feedback loops and tipping points, exploring their significance and their role in complex systems. We will delve into how these loops can shape and influence the behavior and stability of natural and social systems.

Feedback loops are dynamic processes in which the output of a system affects its input, creating a self-reinforcing or self-correcting effect. They can lead to exponential growth, stability, or even abrupt shifts in the behavior of a system. There are two types of feedback loops: positive and negative.

Positive feedback loops occur when the output of a system reinforces or amplifies its initial conditions. This results in exponential growth, amplifying impacts, and accelerating change. An excellent example of a positive feedback loop in the natural world is global warming. As greenhouse gases, such as carbon dioxide, accumulate in the atmosphere due to human activities like burning fossil fuels, they trap more heat from the sun. This increased heat leads to the melting of ice caps and increased water vapor in the atmosphere, both of which further enhance the greenhouse effect. This positive feedback loop intensifies the warming and creates a dangerous cycle that accelerates climate change.

Negative feedback loops, on the other hand, provide stability and resilience to systems by counteracting and self-regulating the deviation from a desired state. They act as mechanisms of control, reducing or reversing changes, and promoting balance. One well-known example of a negative feedback loop is the predator-prey relationship. When the population of a prey species increases, it provides more food for the predators, whose population subsequently increases. However, as the predator population grows, they consume more prey, causing the prey population to decrease. This decline in prey results in less food available for the predators, leading to a decrease in their population. This cycle of population regulation maintains a balance within the ecosystem.

Tipping points, also known as critical thresholds, are the point at which a system undergoes a rapid and irreversible change in behavior or state. They represent a significant shift from one stable state to another and often occur when feedback loops reach a critical intensity. Tipping points can arise in natural and social systems, with profound implications for their functioning and future trajectory. For example, deforestation-driven loss of rainforests can lead to a tipping point where the clearing of trees disrupts rainfall patterns and reduces the capacity for other vegetation to grow. This can result in the transformation of the rainforest ecosystem into a more arid desert-like environment, with far-reaching impacts on biodiversity, climate, and local populations.

Understanding feedback loops and tipping points is crucial for managing complex systems and predicting their behavior. They highlight the non-linear, interconnected nature of these systems, and the importance of identifying indicators and early warning signs of potential shifts. By recognizing the presence and dynamics of feedback loops and tipping points, decision-makers can develop strategies to steer systems towards desirable states or prevent unwanted shifts. In the case of climate change, for instance, tipping points associated with the melting of Arctic ice might trigger irreversible consequences. Recognizing and responding to these tipping points is crucial to avoid catastrophic outcomes.

In conclusion, feedback loops and tipping points play a vital role in shaping the behavior, stability, and resilience of complex systems. Positive feedback loops can drive exponential growth and rapid change, while negative feedback loops promote stability and balance. Tipping points represent critical thresholds where systems undergo irreversible shifts. Understanding these concepts enables us to comprehend and manage the dynamics and risks associated with various systems, from ecosystems to social networks. It serves as a valuable tool for developing strategies to ensure a sustainable and resilient future for our planet and society.

8.1 Understanding Climate Feedback Mechanisms

Thank you for your feedback! I'm glad you found the writing to be long, detailed, and interesting regarding understanding climate feedback mechanisms. Climate feedback mechanisms play a crucial role in the Earth's climate system and can either amplify or dampen the effects of climate change.

Feedback mechanisms occur when changes in one component of the climate system cause further changes, either positive or negative, in other components, thereby creating a feedback loop. These loops can either reinforce or offset the initial change, resulting in either amplification or dampening of the climate effects, respectively.

One of the key feedback mechanisms in the climate system is the ice-albedo feedback. The albedo refers to the reflectivity of a surface, with lighter surfaces reflecting more sunlight than darker surfaces. When ice melts, darker surfaces such as water or land are exposed, which absorb more sunlight and increase temperatures. This leads to further ice melt, creating a positive feedback loop that amplifies climate warming.

Another significant feedback mechanism is the water vapor feedback. As the atmosphere warms, it can hold more water vapor, which is a potent greenhouse gas. This increased water vapor further enhances the greenhouse effect, trapping more heat in the atmosphere and causing more warming. This feedback loop contributes to the majority of the warming projected by climate models.

Other important feedback mechanisms include the cloud feedback, which involves the complex interactions between clouds and radiation, and the carbon cycle feedback. The carbon cycle feedback operates through changes in the uptake and release of carbon dioxide by the biosphere, oceans, and terrestrial systems. Increased carbon dioxide concentrations can enhance plant growth, leading to increased carbon uptake, but can also cause increased decomposition of organic matter, releasing more carbon dioxide back into the atmosphere.

Understanding and quantifying these feedback mechanisms is critical for accurately predicting future climate change and informing mitigation and adaptation strategies. Climate models incorporate various feedback mechanisms to simulate and project future climate scenarios. They consider interactions between the atmosphere, oceans, cryosphere, and ecosystems to capture the complex dynamics of the Earth's climate system.

Overall, comprehending climate feedback mechanisms is crucial for understanding the drivers and impacts of climate change. The interplay between these mechanisms ultimately determines the sensitivity of the climate system to external forcings and the severity of climate change.

8.2 Potential Tipping Points for Global Warming and Ocean Acidification

Global warming and ocean acidification are two major environmental issues facing the planet today, with the potential to cause significant negative impacts on ecosystems and human society. While there is already overwhelming scientific evidence of their existence and the role of human activities in driving them, understanding the potential tipping points for these phenomena is crucial for predicting their future trajectories and developing effective mitigation strategies.

1. Arctic Sea Ice Loss: The Arctic region is particularly susceptible to climate change, and the accelerating loss of sea ice in this area is a key concern. As ice reflects sunlight back into space, the reduction in ice cover is causing increased absorption of solar radiation, leading to amplified warming in the region and beyond. Researchers speculate that an ice-free Arctic in summer could occur within a few decades. This could trigger irreversible changes in atmospheric circulation patterns and disrupt oceanic currents, resulting in altered weather patterns across the globe.

2. Disintegration of Antarctic Ice Sheets: Antarctica holds the largest amount of freshwater on Earth, stored in massive ice sheets. However, there is evidence that these ice sheets are becoming increasingly unstable as temperatures rise. If they were to significantly melt, it would lead to a rapid rise in sea levels that could displace millions of coastal inhabitants worldwide and cause irreparable damage to critical coastal habitats for plants and animals.

3. Rainforest Dieback: Tropical rainforests are vital carbon sinks, absorbing large amounts of atmospheric carbon dioxide (CO_2) and influencing global climate patterns. However, increased drought conditions, wildfires, and deforestation have put these ecosystems at risk. If a tipping point is reached where the loss of rainforest cover is greater than its ability to regrow, it could shift from being a carbon sink to a carbon source. The excessive release of CO_2 into the atmosphere would accelerate global warming.

4. Changes in the Atlantic Meridional Overturning Circulation (AMOC): The AMOC is a vital oceanic conveyor belt that transports warm surface waters from the tropics to the North Atlantic, where they release heat to the atmosphere and then sink to the deep ocean. This circulation plays a critical role in distributing heat globally and affects regional climates, such as the relatively temperate climate in Europe. A tipping point that disrupts or stops the AMOC could have far-reaching consequences, triggering changes in weather patterns, altering precipitation and temperature regimes, and potentially leading to extreme weather events.

5. Collapse of Coral Reefs: Coral reefs provide vital ecosystem services, supporting a wide range of marine life and providing coastal protection. However, they are highly sensitive to changes in water temperature and acidity. Already at risk from coral bleaching due to warming waters, reefs are also threatened by ocean acidification as the absorption of increasing CO2 levels makes the waters more acidic. Once a tipping point is crossed, large-scale coral mortality and subsequent ecosystem collapse may be irreversible, leading to the loss of habitat and biodiversity globally.

6. Methane Release from Permafrost and Hydrates: Methane is a potent greenhouse gas with more significant warming potential than CO2. In frozen ground layers called permafrost and trapped deep under the ocean floor in hydrates, vast amounts of methane are stored. As temperatures rise, there is a risk of releasing these reserves, creating a positive feedback loop that can further amplify global warming. If significant amounts of methane are released, it could accelerate the pace of climate change beyond what current predictions foresee.

7. Ocean Deoxygenation: Global warming is depleting oxygen levels in the oceans, particularly in the oxygen minimum zones, which are critical habitats for many fish and invertebrates. As oxygen declines, marine life will be forced to migrate to more oxygen-rich areas, leading to disruptions in predator-prey relationships and altering ecosystems. If this trend continues and spreads to larger areas of the ocean, it could result in widespread loss of biodiversity and affect the availability of seafood, impacting human societies and economies.

8. Amplified Positive Feedback Cycles: Tipping points could trigger positive feedback cycles where the consequences of global warming and ocean acidification reinforce each other, leading to further warming and acidification.

For instance, as the Earth warms, forests and vegetation could release stored carbon, further exacerbating greenhouse gas emissions. Additionally, as the ocean absorbs more CO2, its capacity to buffer acidification diminishes, making it more vulnerable to further changes. These feedback loops could significantly hasten the pace at which both global warming and ocean acidification occur.

While the exact timing and magnitude of these tipping points remain uncertain, it is clear that we need to take urgent action to mitigate global warming and ocean acidification. It is crucial to implement policies that reduce greenhouse gas emissions, protect and restore key ecosystems, and adopt sustainable practices to prevent reaching these tipping points and safeguard the wellbeing of both nature and our future generations.

8.3 Implications of Feedback Loops on Future Projections

Feedback loops are an essential part of understanding and making future projections. These loops can have significant implications on various systems and can lead to unexpected outcomes. In this article, we will explore the implications of feedback loops on future projections.

1. Amplification: Feedback loops can amplify the effects of certain variables in a system. For example, consider a positive feedback loop in climate change. As temperatures rise, ice caps melt, reducing the Earth's ability to reflect sunlight, which leads to more warming and further melting of ice caps. This amplification effect can make future projections even more extreme than initially anticipated.

2. Destabilization: Feedback loops can also destabilize a system, making it more unpredictable and prone to abrupt changes. Take, for example, a negative feedback loop in the economic system. A decrease in consumer spending leads to a decrease in production, which, in turn, leads to job losses and further decreases in spending. This feedback loop can create a downward spiral and make it difficult to project future economic conditions accurately.

3. Tipping Points: Feedback loops can push systems past critical thresholds known as tipping points. These tipping points represent a point of no return, where a system undergoes a sudden and often irreversible transition. For instance, a positive feedback loop in the spread of infectious diseases can lead to a tipping point where the number of infected individuals increases rapidly, overwhelming healthcare systems and making it difficult to contain the outbreak.

4. Cyclical Patterns: Feedback loops can create cyclical patterns in systems, leading to predictable fluctuations over time. These patterns can be seen in various domains, such as financial markets, climate patterns, or population dynamics. By understanding and analyzing these cycles, future projections can account for these patterns and make forecasts accordingly.

5. Systemic Change: Feedback loops can also drive systemic change in a complex system. A small change in one component can trigger a series of interactions and adjustments throughout the system, leading to a new equilibrium or even a completely different system state. These long-term impacts can significantly alter future projections, especially when dealing with interconnected and dynamic systems.

6. Delayed Responses: Feedback loops can introduce delays in a system's response to changes in input variables. For example, consider the feedback loop between greenhouse gas emissions and climate change. It takes time for the Earth's climate system to respond fully to changes in atmospheric greenhouse gas concentrations. This delayed response can result in underestimated or delayed impacts in future projections, making it challenging to accurately forecast future climate conditions.

In conclusion, feedback loops play a critical role in shaping future projections. Whether it be through amplification, destabilization, tipping points, cyclical patterns, systemic change, or delayed responses, these loops can have significant implications on various systems. Recognizing and understanding these implications is vital for making accurate and reliable future projections in a wide range of fields such as climate science, economics, and public health.

Chapter 9: Mitigation Strategies to Combat Global Warming and Ocean Acidification

Global warming and ocean acidification are two interconnected environmental threats that pose serious consequences for the planet and its inhabitants. As these challenges continue to worsen, it becomes of utmost importance to implement effective mitigation strategies to combat these issues. This chapter provides a detailed and comprehensive overview of various mitigation strategies that can be employed to tackle global warming and ocean acidification. These strategies range from reducing greenhouse gas emissions to promoting renewable energy sources and protecting ecosystems that play a crucial role in climate regulation.

1. Reducing greenhouse gas emissions:

One of the leading causes of global warming and ocean acidification is the excessive release of greenhouse gases into the atmosphere. By reducing the emissions of these gases, we can significantly mitigate the adverse effects on climate and ocean health. This can be achieved through various steps like the promotion of energy-efficient technologies, transitioning to low-carbon transportation systems, and implementing stringent regulations on industrial emissions.

2. Promoting renewable energy sources:

Fossil fuels are the primary sources of greenhouse gas emissions, and their combustion contributes greatly to global warming and ocean acidification. To combat these issues, it is crucial to shift our reliance on renewable energy sources, such as solar, wind, and hydroelectric power. Investing in renewable energy infrastructure, incentivizing their use, and promoting research and development in this field can aid in reducing our carbon footprint and mitigating climate change and ocean acidification.

3. Encouraging energy conservation:

In addition to adopting renewable energy sources, it is important to promote energy conservation practices. Simple steps like turning off lights when not in use, using energy-efficient appliances, and properly insulating buildings can significantly reduce energy consumption and, subsequently, greenhouse gas emissions. Moreover, educational campaigns aimed at raising awareness about energy conservation can play a vital role in encouraging individuals and communities to embrace sustainable lifestyles.

4. Carbon sequestration and storage:

Carbon sequestration refers to the capture and storage of carbon dioxide from the atmosphere to prevent it from contributing to global warming. Different technologies, such as afforestation and reforestation, can help sequester carbon by increasing vegetation cover. Additionally, implementing carbon capture and storage (CCS) technologies in various industries can effectively reduce emissions. These strategies enable the removal of CO2 from the atmosphere, preventing its absorption by the oceans and subsequent acidification.

5. Sustainable agriculture practices:

The agricultural sector is not only a significant contributor to greenhouse gas emissions but also indirectly affects ocean health through fertilizer and pesticide runoff. By adopting sustainable farming methods, such as organic agriculture and precision farming techniques, we can mitigate emissions and reduce the environmental impact. Furthermore, promoting agroforestry and diversification of crop production can enhance carbon sequestration in soils, thus contributing to climate change mitigation.

6. Protecting and restoring ecosystems:

Ecosystems, particularly forests and coastal habitats like coral reefs and mangroves, play a vital role in regulating climate and supporting marine biodiversity. Protecting and restoring these ecosystems can provide substantial mitigation benefits. Forest conservation prevents carbon release through deforestation and supports carbon sequestration. Similarly, restoring coastal habitats can enhance carbon capture from the atmosphere and provide natural buffers against the impacts of ocean acidification.

7. International climate agreements:

Global cooperation is crucial to effectively combat global warming and ocean acidification. International agreements like the Paris Agreement, which aim to limit global temperature increase, provide a framework for countries to collectively address these challenges. Encouraging participation and ensuring compliance with such agreements can strengthen mitigation efforts on a global scale.

MITIGATING GLOBAL WARMING and ocean acidification requires a concerted effort from governments, industries, and individuals. Implementing a combination of strategies like reducing emissions, promoting renewable energy sources, conserving energy, sequestering carbon, adopting sustainable agriculture practices, protecting ecosystems, and adhering to international agreements can bring us closer to a sustainable future. With timely action and commitment, we can mitigate the adverse effects of climate change on our planet and safeguard the health and vitality of our oceans for generations to come.

9.1 Sustainable Energy Sources and Reducing Carbon Emissions

Sustainable energy sources and reducing carbon emissions have become vital considerations as we strive towards a more environmentally conscious world. In this article, we will delve into the topic of sustainable energy sources and examine their positive impact on both the environment and our everyday lives. Additionally, we will explore different strategies and technologies that help reduce carbon emissions, contributing to a more sustainable future.

1. Renewable Energy Sources:

Renewable energy sources harness natural processes that replenish themselves over time. They provide an abundant and clean energy alternative to fossil fuels. Key examples of renewable energy sources include:

a) Solar Power: Solar energy is converted into electricity through the use of photovoltaic (PV) panels. These panels convert sunlight directly into usable electricity and are increasingly cost-effective and efficient. Solar power helps reduce carbon emissions as it generates electricity without burning fossil fuels.

b) Wind Power: Wind turbines capture energy from the wind and convert it into electrical power. As wind is an inexhaustible resource, wind farms are an excellent source of sustainable energy, with no direct carbon emissions.

c) Hydropower: Hydropower involves harnessing energy from flowing water, typically rivers or tides, to generate electricity. Hydroelectric power plants provide a stable and constant source of renewable energy. Unlike fossil fuel power plants, they emit minimal greenhouse gases during operation.

2. Benefits of Sustainable Energy Sources:

Using sustainable energy sources presents numerous advantages for the environment and society. Some of the key benefits include:

a) Reduced Carbon Emissions: Traditional energy sources such as coal and natural gas emit large amounts of greenhouse gases during combustion. By replacing these sources with sustainable alternatives, we can significantly reduce carbon emissions and mitigate climate change.

b) Energy Security and Independence: Relying on renewable energy sources reduces our dependence on fossil fuels, which often originate from politically unstable regions. Using sustainable energy helps promote energy independence and stability.

c) Job Creation and Economic Growth: The renewable energy sector provides opportunities for job creation and economic growth. Investing in sustainable energy sources stimulates local economies and creates long-term employment prospects.

3. Strategies for Reducing Carbon Emissions:

Apart from adopting sustainable energy sources, several strategies focus on minimizing carbon emissions from conventional energy sources:

a) Energy Efficiency: One of the most effective ways to reduce emissions is by improving energy efficiency. Energy-efficient technologies minimize energy wastage and significantly cut down on carbon emissions.

b) Carbon Capture and Storage (CCS): CCS technologies capture carbon dioxide emissions from power plants and industrial activities, preventing them from entering the atmosphere. Captured CO2 is then stored in underground geologic formations, reducing its impact on global warming.

c) Transition to Electric Vehicles (EVs): The transportation sector accounts for a substantial portion of carbon emissions. Shifting to electric vehicles helps reduce these emissions through the use of renewable electricity as a power source.

AS THE WORLD FACES the dire consequences of climate change, transitioning towards sustainable energy sources and reducing carbon emissions has become a necessity. Embracing renewable energy technologies, improving energy efficiency, and employing carbon capture methods are crucial steps to achieving a cleaner, more sustainable future. By collectively adopting these strategies, we can make a significant positive impact on the environment, protect our natural resources, and secure a greener world for generations to come.

9.2 Conservation and Restoration of Marine Ecosystems

Conservation and restoration of marine ecosystems are crucial for the health and well-being of our planet. Marine ecosystems are home to a vast array of plants and animals, and they provide numerous ecosystem services that are essential for human survival. Despite their importance, these ecosystems are being rapidly degraded and destroyed due to various human activities such as pollution, overfishing, and habitat destruction. Therefore, it is imperative that we take action to protect and restore these vital ecosystems.

Conservation of marine ecosystems involves the establishment and management of protected areas like marine sanctuaries, national parks, and marine reserves. These protected areas help to safeguard important habitats and species from destructive practices. They provide a safe haven for marine life to recover and flourish, and they also serve as research sites for scientists to study and understand these complex ecosystems. Marine protected areas often have strict regulations to limit activities like fishing, boating, and diving to minimize human-induced disturbances.

In addition to protected areas, effective marine conservation also requires the implementation of sustainable fishing practices. Overfishing is a major threat to marine ecosystems, as it disrupts food chains and leads to the decline of fish populations. To address this issue, many countries have adopted fisheries management plans and quotas to ensure that fishing activities are sustainable and do not deplete stock sizes. These measures aim to prevent overfishing while allowing for the responsible harvesting of marine resources.

Furthermore, reducing pollution is another essential aspect of marine ecosystem conservation. Pollution from various sources, such as industrial discharges, agricultural run-off, and plastics, can have devastating effects on marine life. It can lead to water contamination, habitat degradation, and harm to marine species. To mitigate pollution, it is crucial to implement stringent regulations and enforce proper waste management practices. This includes the reduction of single-use plastics, the implementation of wastewater treatment systems, and the promotion of eco-friendly practices on land and at sea.

When it comes to the restoration of marine ecosystems, several methods can be employed to help these habitats recover from degradation. One such method is coral reef restoration, which involves the cultivation and transplantation of coral fragments onto damaged reefs. These efforts can help to rebuild coral populations and enhance the overall health and resilience of reefs. Additionally, habitat restoration projects can focus on re-establishing seagrass beds, mangrove forests, and salt marshes, as these habitats provide essential breeding grounds, nurseries, and feeding areas for many marine organisms.

Restoring marine ecosystems also involves active measures to rehabilitate populations of threatened and endangered species. This can include captive breeding and reintroduction programs for species like sea turtles, marine mammals, and seabirds. By helping to increase population numbers, these programs contribute to the overall biodiversity and health of marine ecosystems.

It is important to recognize that the conservation and restoration of marine ecosystems require long-term commitment and collaborative efforts from governments, non-governmental organizations, local communities, and individuals. It is a multifaceted challenge that necessitates a combination of science-based management strategies, policy development, education, and public engagement. Only through collective action and awareness can we hope to safeguard the diversity and resilience of marine ecosystems for future generations.

In conclusion, the conservation and restoration of marine ecosystems are paramount to the well-being of our planet. Protecting these invaluable habitats and their inhabitants from destructive practices is critical to maintaining ecosystem balance and providing essential ecosystem services. Sustainable fishing practices, pollution reduction, protected areas, and species restoration are all key components of comprehensive marine conservation and restoration efforts. By implementing these strategies and working together, we can ensure the long-term health and sustainability of our precious marine ecosystems.

9.3 International Cooperation and Policy Interventions

This section of the document focuses on international cooperation and policy interventions within the context of 9.3, which is concerned with the interplay between sustainable development and peacebuilding. International cooperation and policy interventions play a crucial role in addressing the challenges that arise from the complex interdependencies between sustainable development and peace.

Firstly, it is important to understand the significance of international cooperation in achieving sustainable development and peace. The challenges faced by countries, especially those affected by conflict or strife, cut across national borders and require a collective effort to address effectively.

Through international cooperation, countries can pool together resources, knowledge, and expertise to tackle the underlying issues and promote sustainable solutions. This can involve sharing best practices, providing technical assistance, capacity-building programs, and coordinating efforts on a global or regional scale.

Furthermore, international cooperation fosters a sense of solidarity and builds trust and understanding among nations. This is particularly important in fragile contexts, where conflicts may have deep-rooted historical and social dimensions. By working together towards common goals, countries can overcome political and ideological differences and build stronger relationships based on mutual trust and respect.

Policy interventions are another crucial aspect of international cooperation in 9.3. Policies serve as a roadmap, guiding and directing efforts towards sustainable development and peacebuilding. Effective policies are essential in creating an enabling environment and establishing the necessary preconditions for sustainable development.

Policy interventions can be diverse and may cover a wide range of areas. For example, they can address issues related to governance, peacebuilding, poverty eradication, social inclusion, climate change, and environmental protection, among others. These policies are often interconnected and require a holistic and integrated approach to be effective.

Incorporating a gender perspective in policy interventions is also crucial. Women, as key agents of change, have been increasingly recognized for their contributions to sustainable development and peacebuilding. Gender-responsive policies aim to address the unique needs and challenges faced by women, as well as ensure their meaningful participation in decision-making processes.

Additionally, policy interventions should take into consideration the specific context and needs of the communities they aim to support. The localization of policies is essential in capturing the diversity and complexity of challenges faced by different communities and tailoring interventions accordingly. This includes involving and engaging local actors, such as civil society organizations, community leaders, and indigenous groups, throughout the policy development and implementation process.

To ensure the effectiveness of international cooperation and policy interventions in addressing the interlinkages between sustainable development and peacebuilding, monitoring and evaluation mechanisms should be put in place. This allows for the assessment of progress, identification of gaps and bottlenecks, and adjustment and refinement of policies and interventions as necessary.

In conclusion, international cooperation and policy interventions are crucial in addressing the complexity of 9.3 and achieving sustainable development and peace. Through cooperation, countries can overcome common challenges and work towards shared goals. Policy interventions provide a framework for action, guiding efforts towards sustainable solutions. The inclusion of diverse perspectives, particularly a gender perspective, and localization of policies are also integral to effectively address the unique needs and context of different communities. Monitoring and evaluation mechanisms ensure the continuous improvement and effectiveness of international cooperation and policy interventions.

Chapter 10: Technological Innovations in Addressing Global Warming and Ocean Acidification

Global warming and ocean acidification are two critical environmental challenges the world is currently facing. These issues have far-reaching implications for ecosystems, economies, and human well-being. Over the years, scientists and engineers have been working tirelessly to develop innovative technologies to combat these problems. In this chapter, we will explore some of the technological innovations that have been developed to address global warming and ocean acidification.

Technological Innovations to Combat Global Warming:

1. Renewable Energy Technologies:

One of the main contributors to global warming is the burning of fossil fuels for energy production. To mitigate this, renewable energy technologies have emerged as a game-changer. Solar, wind, hydroelectric, and geothermal power generating systems have been developed to harness clean and abundant sources of energy. These technologies reduce greenhouse gas emissions and provide sustainable energy solutions.

2. Carbon Capture and Storage (CCS):

CCS technology involves capturing carbon dioxide (CO_2) emitted from power plants and industrial facilities and storing it underground or repurposing it for industrial use. CCS has the potential to significantly reduce CO_2 emissions and prevent their release into the atmosphere. However, more research is required to improve this technology and make it cost-effective.

3. Bioenergy:

Bioenergy technologies involve the production of energy from biomass (organic matter) such as agricultural residues, forestry waste, or energy crops. Biomass can be converted into heat, electricity, or liquid fuels. By utilizing bioenergy, we can reduce the reliance on fossil fuels and decrease carbon emissions.

Technological Innovations to Tackle Ocean Acidification:

1. Artificial Reef Restoration Systems:

Artificial reefs are designed structures that mimic natural coral reefs and provide habitats for marine life. These structures can be made from various materials, including concrete, steel, and fiberglass. Artificial reefs help restore damaged ecosystems affected by ocean acidification, offering new habitats for fish and protecting vulnerable marine organisms.

2. Ocean Alkalinization:

Ocean alkalinization involves adding alkaline substances to seawater to counteract its acidity. By increasing the pH and buffering capacity of ocean water, alkalinization can mitigate the impacts of ocean acidification. This innovative technology requires further research to better understand its long-term effects on marine ecosystems.

3. Blue Carbon Projects:

Blue carbon refers to the carbon stored within coastal ecosystems like mangroves, seagrasses, and salt marshes. These ecosystems have high carbon sequestration potential, helping to mitigate climate change. Blue carbon projects aim to protect and restore these habitats, enhancing their ability to absorb and store carbon while providing important ecological benefits.

TECHNOLOGICAL INNOVATIONS have showcased great potential in addressing global warming and ocean acidification. Strategic investment in research and development is essential for further improvement and widespread deployment of these technologies. As the world unites to combat these urgent challenges, innovative approaches will play a vital role in preserving the planet's health for future generations. Through global collaboration and continued advancement in technology, we can effectively address the threats posed by global warming and ocean acidification.

10.1 Emerging Technologies for Carbon Capture and Storage

Emerging technologies for carbon capture and storage (CCS) have gained increasing attention in recent years as an important tool to address climate change. These technologies aim to capture carbon dioxide (CO_2) emissions from various industrial processes and store them in a secure manner, preventing them from entering the atmosphere and contributing to global warming.

One of the emerging technologies in CCS is the development of advanced materials for carbon capture. Traditional CCS methods involve the use of solvents, which can be costly and energy-intensive. However, recent research and development efforts have focused on creating advanced materials, such as metal-organic frameworks (MOFs) and porous carbon materials, that can adsorb CO_2 more effectively and efficiently. These materials have a high surface area and can selectively capture CO_2 when it comes into contact with them. This technology has the potential to significantly reduce the costs and energy requirements associated with CCS.

Another promising technology for CCS is direct air capture (DAC). Unlike traditional CCS methods that capture CO_2 emissions at the source, DAC allows for the removal of CO_2 directly from the atmosphere. DAC uses large-scale devices that contain materials with high CO_2 adsorption capacity, which capture CO_2 molecules as air passes through them. Once the CO_2 is captured, it can be stored underground or utilized for various purposes, such as enhanced oil recovery or the production of synthetic fuels. While DAC is still in its early stages of development, it holds great potential for removing large amounts of CO_2 from the atmosphere and helping to mitigate climate change.

In addition to advanced materials and direct air capture, there are other emerging technologies for CCS in various stages of development. These include bioenergy with CCS (BECCS), which involves the combustion of biomass for energy generation and the subsequent capture and storage of CO_2 emissions. BECCS has the potential to achieve negative emissions, as the biomass used in the process absorbs CO2 as it grows, effectively removing CO2 from the atmosphere. Other technologies include carbon mineralization, which involves the conversion of CO2 into stable minerals through chemical reactions, and carbon capture and utilization (CCU), where captured CO2 is transformed into value-added products, such as chemicals, plastics, or construction materials.

Despite the significant promise of these emerging technologies, there are still several challenges that need to be addressed for their widespread deployment. One of the main challenges is the high cost of implementation. CCS technologies require large-scale infrastructure for carbon capture, transport, and storage, which can be expensive to build and maintain. Additionally, the long-term storage of captured CO2 underground or in other secure locations requires careful monitoring and regulation to ensure leakage does not occur.

Another challenge is the limited scale at which these technologies are currently deployed. While some pilot projects exist, scaling up these technologies to a commercial level is still a major hurdle. This relates to the financial and policy framework necessary to incentivize CCS deployment, as well as public acceptance and awareness of the benefits and safety of these technologies.

In conclusion, emerging technologies for carbon capture and storage hold great potential for mitigating greenhouse gas emissions and addressing climate change. Advanced materials for carbon capture, direct air capture, bioenergy with CCS, carbon mineralization, and carbon capture and utilization are at the forefront of research and development efforts in this field. However, challenges such as cost, scale, and public acceptance need to be overcome for these technologies to have significant impact. Continued research, development, and policy support are crucial for the successful deployment of emerging CCS technologies.

10.2 Adaptation Strategies for Vulnerable Coastal Communities

Adaptation Strategies for Vulnerable Coastal Communities

Coastal areas are particularly vulnerable to the impacts of climate change, including sea-level rise, increased storm frequency and intensity, and coastal erosion. These changes can threaten the very existence of coastal communities, displacing populations and causing significant economic losses. In order to mitigate these risks and enhance resilience, it is crucial for these communities to adopt adaptation strategies. Here, we will discuss 10.2 of these strategies in detail.

1. Elevation and Relocation: One key adaptation strategy is to elevate buildings and infrastructure to protect them from flooding and storm surges. In some cases, relocation of vulnerable buildings and communities might be necessary to safer areas.

2. Coastal Defense and Protection: The implementation of coastal defenses, such as sea walls and breakwaters, can help protect coastal infrastructure and reduce the risk of erosion and inundation.

3. Beach Nourishment: Adding sand to eroded beaches helps increase their width and height, providing a natural barrier against wave impacts and reducing coastal erosion.

4. Wetlands Restoration: Restoring wetlands, such as salt marshes and mangroves, can attenuate wave energy and protect coastal areas from storms and erosion.

5. Dune Establishment: Creating or restoring coastal dunes helps to act as natural buffers against storm surges and erosion, as they dissipate wave energy.

6. Nature-based Solutions: Implementing nature-based solutions, such as living shorelines and oyster reefs, not only provides protection against erosion and storm surge but often offers other co-benefits like water filtration and habitat creation.

7. Integrated Coastal Zone Management (ICZM): Adopting an ICZM approach can help coordinate adaptation efforts among government agencies, stakeholders, and communities to ensure the sustainable and effective management of coastal resources.

8. Early Warning Systems (EWS): Establishing robust early warning systems can save lives and reduce damage by providing timely alerts for coastal communities in the path of an approaching storm or other hazardous events.

9. Climate-Resilient Infrastructure: Investing in climate-resilient infrastructure, such as stormwater management systems and flood-proof roads, can significantly reduce vulnerability to climate-related hazards.

10. Community Engagement and Education: Actively engaging coastal communities in the planning and implementation of adaptation strategies enhances social resilience by improving awareness and understanding of climate risks, fostering a sense of ownership, and encouraging local knowledge and expertise.

These 10.2 adaptation strategies highlight some of the ways in which vulnerable coastal communities can enhance their resilience in the face of climate change. A combination of multiple strategies customized for specific regions and community needs is often necessary for effective adaptation. It is crucial for governments, communities, and international organizations to work together to prioritize adaptation efforts, allocate resources, and implement these strategies to safeguard the people and the environment in these vulnerable coastal areas.

10.3 Promising Breakthroughs in Ocean Regeneration

The world's oceans are facing a multitude of challenges today, from overfishing to plastic pollution and climate change. As these issues intensify, the urgent need for innovative solutions to regenerate and protect our oceans becomes increasingly evident. Fortunately, scientists and researchers are making significant breakthroughs in various fields, providing some hope for a brighter future. This article discusses 10.3 important promising breakthroughs that hold great potential to address the challenges faced by our oceans.

1. Artificial Reefs:

Artificial reef systems play a vital role in mitigating the effects of habitat loss and enhancing marine biodiversity. Researchers are developing innovative designs using environmentally friendly materials and human-made structures that create habitats for various marine life forms. By restoring damaged ecosystems, these artificial reefs offer humans a chance to counterbalance the negative impacts of coastal development and other human activities.

2. Marine Spatial Planning:

Marine scientists and policymakers are recognizing the importance of implementing strategic planning to establish areas designated for certain activities. The concept of marine spatial planning allows for sustainable, balanced ecosystems, allocating zones for commercial fishing, conservation, recreation, and renewable energy development. Such planning helps mitigate conflicts of interest and promotes responsible ocean use.

3. Seaweed Farming:

The growth of seaweed farming has gained momentum due to its multifaceted role in ocean regeneration. Seaweed farming not only acts as a carbon sink, absorbing atmospheric CO_2, but it also holds potential as a sustainable source of biofuel, food, and animal feed. Furthermore, seaweeds can remove excessive nutrients from coastal waters, contributing to mitigating harmful algal blooms.

4. 3D Printing coral reefs:

Corals, crucial for supporting diverse marine ecosystems, have been extensively damaged due to climate change and other factors. Researchers have proposed 3D printing techniques as a way to repair or rebuild damaged reefs by replicating intricate coral structures. By printing artificial corals using materials compatible with natural ones, scientists are hopeful that damaged reefs can regain their structural integrity.

5. Ocean Plastic Cleanup:

With millions of tons of plastic waste polluting our oceans, cleaning up this debris is a daunting task. However, breakthrough technologies such as floating garbage collectors and specially designed nets are being deployed to remove plastic waste efficiently. Innovative systems that convert plastic waste into usable products offer a dual solution of cleaner oceans and sustainable material production.

6. Artificial Intelligence for Sustainable Fishing:

To combat overfishing and preserve fish stocks, researchers are employing artificial intelligence algorithms in fishing practices. Through machine learning, AI can contribute to efficient tracking of fish populations, determining optimum catch limits, and improving fishing gear technology. This potential revolution in sustainable fishing practices aims to strike a balance between fisheries and ecosystem conservation.

7. Hydrothermal Vent Exploration:

Hydrothermal vents, previously deemed inhospitable and inaccessible, are now being explored for important ecological discoveries and novel genetic resources. Researchers are studying these unique deep-sea ecosystems to understand their potential impact on climate regulation and identify bioactive compounds that hold promises for medical and industrial applications.

8. Hydrogen Fuel From Algae:

Researchers are developing collective solutions by using algae to produce hydrogen fuel, presenting a sustainable alternative to fossil fuels. Algae possess high rates of productivity, absorbing CO_2 in the process, making them a promising candidate for fuel production. This breakthrough could revolutionize the energy industry, reduce carbon emissions, and promote sustainable practices.

9. Coral Bleaching Remediation:

Coral bleaching, caused by rising ocean temperatures, has devastated coral reefs worldwide. Promising research is being conducted utilizing "sunscreen" for corals, which involves spreading a biodegradable substance onto the ocean surface to block harmful UV rays from reaching the delicate coral organisms. This breakthrough technique aims to minimize coral mortality and promote reef recovery.

10. Marine Protected Areas:

Acknowledging the importance of conserving marine biodiversity and habitats, initiatives to establish marine protected areas (MPAs) are gaining traction worldwide. MPAs serve as conservation hubs, ensuring the preservation of critical ecosystems and species. These protected areas allow marine populations to thrive and recover from human-induced pollution and disturbances.

WHILE THE CHALLENGES faced by our oceans are vast, these 10.3 promising breakthroughs in ocean regeneration offer hope for a more sustainable future. Through the concerted efforts of scientists, policymakers, and individuals, we can reverse the negative impacts on our oceans and pave the way for an environment where marine life can flourish once more. By prioritizing sustainable practices, technological innovation, and collaborative decision-making, we can ensure a healthy and vibrant ocean ecosystem for generations to come.

Chapter 11: The Role of Public Awareness and Education

Public awareness and education play a pivotal role in shaping society's attitudes, behaviors, and responses in various domains. In the context of this chapter, we will explore their significance in promoting understanding and action related to important issues, such as health, environment, social justice, and more. This chapter aims to highlight the positive impact of public awareness and education while emphasizing the need for well-informed citizens to create a more equitable and sustainable world.

The Power of Public Awareness:

Public awareness campaigns have been successful in fostering positive change by disseminating information, generating interest, and engaging the masses. Whether it's raising awareness about the symptoms of a particular health condition or promoting a behavioral change for environmental conservation, public awareness initiatives provide a platform for information-sharing and dialogue. By creating a buzz and capturing the public's attention, these campaigns can motivate individuals to take action and influence policymakers to implement necessary changes.

In the medical field, public awareness has been instrumental in tackling stigmatization and societal barriers associated with certain illnesses. Human immunodeficiency virus (HIV) and mental health disorders are just two examples of conditions that have benefited immensely from public awareness efforts. By destigmatizing these illnesses and improving access to resources and support networks, these initiatives have ensured better outcomes for affected individuals and society as a whole.

Public Awareness in Environmental Conservation:

Environmental issues have gained considerable attention in recent years, thanks to effective public awareness campaigns. Concerns over climate change, pollution, deforestation, and other environmental challenges have mobilized individuals, communities, and governments to adopt eco-friendly practices, conservation efforts, and sustainable policies. These campaigns disseminate knowledge on the importance of protecting ecosystems, conserving resources, and reducing waste, empowering individuals to make conscious choices that benefit the planet.

In addition to individual actions, collective efforts are pivotal in addressing environmental challenges. Public awareness campaigns promote grassroots movements, community participation, and engagement with policymakers. By rallying support and initiatives at different levels, public awareness facilitates systemic change and influences decision-making processes.

Empowering Marginalized Communities:

Information and education are vital tools for empowering marginalized communities and promoting social justice. By raising awareness about systemic inequalities, discrimination, and bias, public education can challenge long-standing stereotypes and work towards dismantling oppressive systems. Public awareness campaigns have played a critical role in advancing civil rights movements, women's rights, LGBTQ+ rights, and many other social justice causes.

Efforts towards inclusivity and diversity are further strengthened by public awareness and education programs. By highlighting the contributions, experiences, and struggles of underrepresented communities, these campaigns help build empathy, understanding, and respect among individuals from diverse backgrounds. Through storytelling, art, media, and dialogue, public awareness cultivates an environment where everyone's identities and voices are valued and celebrated.

Challenges and Future Considerations:

While public awareness and education initiatives have yielded positive outcomes in many areas, they also face certain challenges. The proliferation of misinformation in the digital age poses a significant obstacle. Misleading or false information can easily spread, causing confusion, hindering well-informed decision-making, and impacting public discourse. Comprehensive fact-checking, media literacy, and critical thinking skills are essential to navigate this complex landscape.

Moreover, creating sustainable, long-term impact requires a holistic approach that involves continuous education and engagement. Public awareness campaigns should not be treated as isolated events but rather as part of a broader framework that involves ongoing education through various channels, including formal education systems, community programs, and digital platforms.

PUBLIC AWARENESS AND education platforms have the potential to shape public opinion, promote behavioral change, and contribute to vital issues such as health, environment, and social justice. By disseminating accurate information, challenging misconceptions, and encouraging dialogue, public awareness campaigns empower individuals to make informed decisions and catalyze positive change. Through long-term, sustained efforts, these initiatives can foster a society that is better equipped to tackle prevailing challenges and create a more equitable and sustainable world for all.

11.1 Importance of Raising Public consciousness

The importance of raising public consciousness cannot be overstated. In a society where individuals are constantly bombarded with information, it is crucial for people to be aware, mindful, and informed about the world around them. Raising public consciousness not only encourages critical thinking, but it also promotes social responsibility, empathy, and engagement.

One of the primary reasons why raising public consciousness is important is because it fosters informed decision-making. In a world where fake news and misinformation run rampant, it is vital for individuals to possess the ability to distinguish between reliable sources and misleading information. By raising public consciousness, people are empowered to critically evaluate information, challenge biases, and make well-informed choices that benefit themselves and their communities.

Furthermore, when individuals are aware and mindful, it promotes social responsibility. People become more cognizant of the impact their actions have on the world. They are more likely to consider the environmental, social, and economic implications of their choices. Raising public consciousness about issues such as climate change, inequality, and poverty helps individuals recognize their own role in these problems and motivates them to be part of the solution.

Empathy is another crucial element that is cultivated through public consciousness. When people are aware of the struggles and challenges that others face, they are more inclined to be compassionate and understanding. Raising public consciousness about social injustices, discrimination, and marginalized communities opens the door for dialogue, understanding, and action. This empathy not only leads to a more inclusive and compassionate society, but also drives initiatives for social change.

Public consciousness also plays a significant role in encouraging civic engagement. When people are informed, they are more likely to participate in democratic processes, engage in activism, and advocate for their beliefs. Raising public consciousness about political issues, human rights, and civic duties empowers individuals to take an active stance in shaping their communities and driving positive change.

Moreover, raising public consciousness helps build a sense of community and shared values. When individuals are aware of the challenges faced by their neighbors, they are more likely to come together and support one another. They recognize the importance of collaboration, solidarity, and collective action. By raising public consciousness, communities can build social capital, fostering a sense of belonging and common purpose.

In conclusion, raising public consciousness is of utmost importance for our society. It enables individuals to make informed decisions, encourages social responsibility, cultivates empathy, promotes civic engagement, and builds strong communities. By investing in initiatives that raise public consciousness, we can create a more knowledgeable, empathetic, and socially conscious society that seeks to drive positive change and contribute to the betterment of all.

11.2 Communications Strategies for Effective Engagement

Effective communication is crucial for any organization to achieve its goals and objectives. Without proper communication, there will be misunderstandings and conflicts which can hinder progress and result in inefficient operations. That is why organizations need to develop comprehensive communication strategies that foster effective engagement with various stakeholders.

One key aspect of communication strategies is to clearly define the target audience. Different stakeholders have different needs and expectations, so it is essential to tailor communication to their specific requirements. For example, when communicating with employees, the language used should be simple and straightforward, while communications with investors may require more technical and financial knowledge.

Another important component of effective communication strategies is to utilize multiple channels. Nowadays, there are numerous ways to reach out to stakeholders, including email, newsletters, social media platforms, and face-to-face meetings. By using different channels, organizations can ensure that their messages are delivered to stakeholders through platforms they are most comfortable with.

In addition to different channels, organizations should also consider the frequency of communication. Regular updates and timely responses to inquiries are crucial in maintaining effective engagement. This includes responding to emails in a prompt manner, publishing regular newsletters, and organizing scheduled meetings or town hall sessions with employees.

To enhance engagement through communication, it is essential for organizations to actively listen to stakeholders. This means addressing concerns, considering feedback, and being open to suggestions and ideas. By creating a culture of open communication, organizations can build trust and rapport with stakeholders, ultimately leading to stronger engagement.

Furthermore, organizations should also consider the use of visual aids when communicating complex information. Visual aids, such as charts and graphs, can make data more digestible and easily understandable. This is particularly relevant when communicating with external stakeholders, such as customers or investors, who may not have detailed knowledge of the organization's operations.

Lastly, communication strategies for effective engagement should be continuously evaluated and adapted. Organizations should regularly assess the impact of their communication efforts, solicit feedback from stakeholders, and make changes based on the results. This ongoing evaluation process will help organizations identify new opportunities, rectify any flaws in communication, and ensure continuous improvement.

In conclusion, developing effective communication strategies is crucial for organizations to achieve effective engagement with stakeholders. By clearly defining target audiences, utilizing multiple channels, actively listening, utilizing visual aids, and regularly evaluating efforts, organizations can foster strong relationships and enhance their overall operations. Communication is the key to success, and organizations that prioritize effective engagement will be well-positioned for future growth and success.

11.3 Educational Initiatives to Encourage Environmental Stewardship

Environmental stewardship refers to the responsible use and protection of the Earth's natural resources. It involves taking action to conserve the environment, promote sustainability, and raise awareness about the importance of protecting the planet for future generations. Educational initiatives play a crucial role in encouraging environmental stewardship among individuals and communities.

1. Environmental Awareness Campaigns: Schools and organizations often organize campaigns to raise awareness about environmental issues. These campaigns may include public service announcements, posters, and workshops that educate people about the consequences of their actions on the environment. By highlighting the impact of pollution, deforestation, and climate change, these educational initiatives help individuals understand the urgent need for environmental stewardship.

2. Environmental Science Programs: Many educational institutions offer environmental science programs that emphasize the importance of sustainable practices and help students develop a deep understanding of ecological processes. By providing hands-on experiences in studying the environment, these programs enable students to become familiar with conservation techniques and ecological principles.

3. Eco-clubs and Green Committees: Many schools create eco-clubs and committees that bring students together to work on environmental initiatives. These student-led groups organize tree planting drives, recycling programs, and clean-up campaigns in their schools and communities. By actively involving students in such initiatives, these clubs instill a sense of responsibility and commitment towards environmental stewardship from a young age.

4. Nature-based Education: Outdoor education programs take students outside the classroom and into nature, allowing them to experience the beauty of the environment firsthand. By participating in activities like nature hikes,

camping, and field trips to natural reserves, students develop a deep connection and appreciation for nature. This connection often leads to a greater inclination towards protecting the environment and practicing sustainable behaviors in their lives.

5. Integration of Environmental Topics in Curriculum: Incorporating environmental topics into various subjects' curricula encourages students to think critically about environmental issues and their solutions. When students learn about biodiversity loss in biology or analyze the impact of industrialization on climate change in economics, they gain a holistic understanding of the intersections between various environmental issues and human activities.

6. Environmental Competitions and Challenges: Encouraging healthy competition through environmental competitions and challenges can motivate individuals to adopt environmentally friendly practices. Competitions like eco-innovation challenges, poster-making competitions, and essay contests can inspire students to think creatively and propose sustainable solutions to environmental problems. These initiatives not only foster talent but also create a sense of camaraderie and enthusiasm among participants.

7. Environmental Guest Speakers and Workshops: Inviting experts to deliver talks and conduct workshops on environmental topics exposes students to a broader perspective on environmental issues. These sessions provide insights into real-world challenges and highlight the role that individuals and communities can play in addressing them. Guest speakers and workshops can inspire students to take action and become environmentally responsible citizens.

8. Partnerships with Environmental Organizations: Collaborating with environmental organizations allows educational institutions to tap into their expertise and resources. Through partnerships, schools can access educational materials, grants, and training programs that help integrate environmental stewardship into their curriculum, promote sustainable practices, and engage students in environmental initiatives.

9. Recycling and Waste Management Programs: Promoting recycling and waste management programs in schools and communities encourages individuals to adopt eco-friendly habits. Educational initiatives that educate students about proper waste segregation and recycling processes not only

reduce the environmental impact of waste but also instill lifelong habits of responsible consumption and waste management.

10. Environmental Field Trips: Field trips to environmental sites, such as national parks, wildlife reserves, or organic farms, allow students to witness sustainable practices firsthand. These field trips provide real-life examples of environmental stewardship in action, inspiring students to value and replicate such practices in their own lives.

11. Community Engagement Projects: Encouraging students to participate in community engagement projects promotes environmental stewardship on a larger scale. By organizing activities like community clean-ups, tree plantations, or awareness drives, educational institutions can help students contribute positively to their local communities, fostering a sense of ownership and responsibility towards the environment.

In conclusion, educational initiatives are fundamental in encouraging environmental stewardship. Through raising awareness, promoting hands-on experiences, integrating environmental topics, fostering partnerships, and engaging students in various activities, educational initiatives play a crucial role in shaping environmentally responsible citizens who care for the planet and take action to protect it.

Chapter 12: Economic and Societal Impacts of Global Warming and Ocean Acidification

The daunting consequences of global warming and ocean acidification have become increasingly evident in recent years. The accelerating rise in global temperatures and the acidification of our oceans have significant economic and societal implications. Understanding the depth and complexity of these impacts is crucial for formulating effective policies and mitigating further damage. In this chapter, we explore the economic and societal ramifications of these intertwined phenomena, shedding light on the challenges they present to our world.

Economic Impacts

1. Agriculture:

Global warming has profound implications for our agricultural systems. Changing climate patterns, increased frequency of extreme weather events, and shifts in precipitation can lead to declines in crop yields and quality. These disruptions expose farmers to greater risks, threaten food security, and strain global economies. Additionally, changes in temperature and rainfall distribution can disrupt pollination patterns, reducing the productivity of key crops like fruits and vegetables.

2. Fisheries:

Ocean acidification poses a significant threat to marine ecosystems, impacting fish populations and ultimately inhibiting fishing industries. Certain species like oysters, clams, and coral reefs are especially vulnerable to acidic waters, compromising their growth, reproduction, and overall survival. This depletion of fish stocks not only undermines the livelihoods of fishermen but also jeopardizes food supplies for communities that heavily rely on seafood.

3. Tourism:

Warmer temperatures and rising sea levels can diminish the appeal of numerous tourist destinations. Iconic sites such as coastal regions, coral reefs, and polar landscapes are particularly sensitive to climate change impacts.

Consequently, dwindling tourism revenues result in economic instability for destinations that heavily depend on this industry. Moreover, extreme weather events, intensified by global warming, disrupt travel plans and heighten risks for both travelers and hospitality sectors.

4. Infrastructure:

The physical infrastructure upon which our societies depend is at risk from the adverse effects of global warming. Sea-level rise, more frequent and severe storms, and widespread droughts threaten the stability and functionality of roads, bridges, buildings, and energy systems. Rebuilding or fortifying infrastructure can impose significant financial burdens on communities already grappling with the costs of natural disasters and their aftermaths.

5. Health:

The ramifications of global warming and ocean acidification also extend to human health. Increased heat waves can lead to heat-related illnesses and fatalities, disproportionately impacting vulnerable populations such as the elderly and those living in urban environments. Additionally, the spread of infectious diseases, such as malaria and dengue fever, can be facilitated by expanding ranges of disease-carrying vectors, like mosquitoes. The strain on healthcare systems and the economic burden of treating and preventing these illnesses further exacerbate the societal impacts.

Societal Impacts

1. Displacement of Populations:

As coastal areas experience sea-level rise and enhanced storm surges, communities inhabiting these regions face the potential relocation. This displacement can result in social unrest, loss of cultural heritage, and strained public resources as governments grapple with the challenge of accommodating environmental refugees. Furthermore, indigenous communities reliant on the natural resources in these vulnerable areas face severe disruptions to their traditional ways of life.

2. Refugee Crises and Conflicts:

Global warming and its economic impacts can exacerbate existing social and geopolitical tensions and lead to mass displacement of people, triggering waves of migration and potentially escalating conflicts. Competition over dwindling resources, including water and arable land, can ignite disputes and create refugee crises, posing significant challenges for economies, security, and stability worldwide.

3. Inequality:

Global warming and ocean acidification have the potential to worsen existing societal inequalities. Historically disadvantaged groups, such as low-income communities and marginalized populations, often bear the brunt of climate change impacts, lacking resources to adapt or recover. These disparities can deepen as vulnerable societies face increasing economic hardships, limited access to healthcare, and limited capacity to cope with environmental upheavals.

4. Mental Health:

The psychological toll of living in a world ravaged by global warming cannot be underestimated. Studies show a correlation between climate change and increased mental health issues, including anxiety, depression, and post-traumatic stress disorder. Uncertain futures, dislocation, and loss associated with climate-related events contribute to mental distress, particularly among populations directly exposed to environmental hazards.

THE ECONOMIC AND SOCIETAL impacts of global warming and ocean acidification are far-reaching and multifaceted. They extend beyond mere environmental concerns, with potential consequences for agricultural productivity, fisheries, tourism, infrastructure stability, human health, social unrest, and pattern of migration, among others. Addressing these impacts necessitates strong international cooperation, innovative policies, and transformative actions. Recognizing the severity of these challenges and taking proactive measures is essential in safeguarding our economic well-being and social cohesion in a warming world.

12.1 Evaluating the Economic Costs of Climate Change

In order to effectively address climate change and develop appropriate policies and strategies, it is crucial to evaluate the economic costs associated with it. Understanding the economic impacts of climate change allows policymakers and stakeholders to make informed decisions and prioritize actions that maximize benefits and minimize costs. Evaluating the economic costs of climate change involves a comprehensive and detailed analysis of various factors, such as the direct and indirect costs, regional disparities, and long-term implications.

One of the primary components of assessing the economic costs of climate change is estimating the direct costs incurred due to climate-related events and phenomena. These events, such as heatwaves, floods, hurricanes, and droughts, can lead to damages to infrastructure, loss of lives, homes, and livelihoods, as well as increased healthcare expenses and rehabilitation costs. Quantifying these direct costs is essential for understanding the immediate impacts and developing effective mitigation and adaptation strategies. Economic models and techniques are used to estimate direct costs, including market-based approaches like replacement and repair costs, as well as non-market approaches such as the willingness to pay for climate change adaptations.

While direct costs are tangible and often more easily quantifiable, indirect costs are equally important but harder to measure. Indirect costs include productivity losses, disruptions in supply chains, loss of ecosystem services, and impacts on sectors like agriculture, tourism, and energy. For example, a decrease in agricultural productivity due to changing climate patterns directly affects food production, availability, and prices. These indirect costs can have wide-ranging and long-lasting effects on key sectors of the economy and societal well-being. Assessing and incorporating indirect costs into economic evaluations provide a more comprehensive understanding of the true economic impacts of climate change.

Furthermore, evaluating the economic costs of climate change necessitates considering regional disparities. The impacts of climate change are not evenly distributed; regions and countries that are more vulnerable and less equipped to withstand climatic changes bear a greater burden. These disparities stem from differences in exposure, susceptibility, adaptive capacity, and economic development. For instance, developing nations, with limited resources and infrastructure, often face more severe economic consequences compared to their developed counterparts. Regional assessments help policymakers identify areas in urgent need of support, aid, and targeted actions, fostering global cooperation and responsibility sharing.

In addition to current economic costs, understanding the long-term implications of climate change is of paramount importance. Climate change is a multi-decadal phenomenon with consequences that will extend well into the future. By evaluating the long-term costs of climate change, policymakers can identify the need for preventive measures, investments in research and development, and policy adjustments that will yield greater benefits in the long run. Considerations of long-term costs emphasize the importance of early action and highlight the potential economic benefits associated with reducing greenhouse gas emissions and promoting sustainable practices.

In conclusion, evaluating the economic costs of climate change encompasses a wide range of factors and considerations. Assessing both direct and indirect costs, addressing regional disparities, and incorporating long-term implications provide a comprehensive understanding of the economic impacts of climate change. By integrating economic evaluations into climate change strategies and policies, decision-makers can prioritize efforts that are cost-effective, supportive of vulnerable regions, and promote sustainable and resilient development.

12.2 Implications on Human Health and Livelihoods

Implications on human health and livelihoods are at the forefront when discussing the effects of various factors on our well-being. In the context of this writing, we will delve into the extensive and fascinating information surrounding this topic. Brace yourself for a lengthy journey into the intricate web of implications.

First and foremost, it is critical to acknowledge the profound impact that human health has on our overall well-being. Health encompasses not only our physical state but also our mental and emotional states. Research has consistently shown that numerous environmental, lifestyle, and genetic factors can influence our health outcomes.

One key factor that has been extensively studied is the environment. The environment plays a crucial role in determining exposure to various pollutants, toxins, and hazardous substances. Pollution, in its various forms such as air pollution, water pollution, and soil contamination, has a direct impact on our health.

Air pollution, for instance, has been linked to respiratory diseases such as asthma, chronic obstructive pulmonary disease (COPD), and even lung cancer. Fine particulate matter and harmful gases emitted from vehicles, factories, and power plants contribute to the deterioration of air quality and subsequently human health.

Water pollution, on the other hand, poses grave threats to human health. Contamination of water sources by chemical pollutants, pathogens, and heavy metals can result in gastrointestinal infections, cholera outbreaks, and even long-term effects like cancer. Access to clean and safe drinking water and proper sanitation facilities are fundamental prerequisites for a healthy population.

Another crucial aspect of human health is lifestyle. Health behaviors such as physical activity, diet choices, and substance use profoundly impact our well-being. Sedentary lifestyles, characterized by a lack of exercise and excessive sitting, contribute to the onset of chronic conditions like obesity, diabetes, and cardiovascular diseases. Eating diets high in processed foods, sugar, and unhealthy fats can lead to weight gain and related health issues. Furthermore, substance abuse, whether drugs, alcohol, or tobacco, can wreak havoc on our physical and mental health.

Additionally, genetics plays a critical role in our health outcomes. Genetic predispositions can increase vulnerability to certain diseases or influence the response to treatments. However, it is important to note that genetics alone does not dictate our health. Lifestyle choices and environmental factors also play considerable roles.

When considering the implications on livelihoods, it is essential to recognize the interplay between human health and economic productivity. An unhealthy population directly impacts economies on various levels. Populations suffering from high rates of morbidity and mortality cannot contribute fully to economic activities, leading to reduced productivity and economic output. Healthcare costs can also escalate, burdening individuals, businesses, and governments.

Moreover, poor health can exacerbate inequality. Marginalized populations, who often face higher levels of health disparities, are further disadvantaged by limited access to healthcare, education, and economic opportunities. This vicious cycle perpetuates social and economic inequities, affecting the overall well-being of these populations.

In conclusion, the implications of various factors on human health and livelihoods are far-reaching and multi-faceted. Factors such as environmental pollution, lifestyle choices, and genetics all intricately affect our health outcomes. Moreover, a healthy population is central to a thriving economy and the promotion of social well-being. It is imperative for policymakers, individuals, and communities to take collective action to mitigate the negative impacts on human health and address the underlying sociopolitical factors that contribute to health disparities. By doing so, we can move closer to a world where every individual has the ability to lead a healthy and productive life.

12.3 Equity and Social Justice Considerations

Equity and social justice considerations play a crucial role in various domains of society, including education, healthcare, employment, and criminal justice. These considerations are vital to ensure fairness, equal opportunities, and the protection of marginalized and underprivileged communities.

In the realm of education, equity and social justice considerations aim to promote equal access to quality education for all students, regardless of their socio-economic background, race, ethnicity, or other demographic factors. This includes addressing issues such as funding disparities, school segregation, and the achievement gap.

For instance, a focus on equity and social justice may involve allocating additional resources, such as funding and support services, to schools that serve disadvantaged communities. It may also involve implementing policies to diversify teaching staff and curriculum, ensuring that students from all backgrounds see their culture and experiences represented in their education.

In the healthcare sector, equity and social justice considerations are crucial to tackle disparities in access to healthcare services and health outcomes. These considerations involve understanding and addressing the social and economic factors that contribute to health disparities among different populations.

For example, in order to promote equity in healthcare, policies may be put in place to expand healthcare coverage to low-income individuals and communities, increase the number of healthcare providers in under-resourced areas, and invest in preventive healthcare measures to reduce preventable illnesses.

Employment is another area where equity and social justice considerations are of utmost importance. These considerations encompass promoting equal pay for equal work, combating discriminatory hiring practices, and creating inclusive and diverse work environments.

For instance, organizations may implement policies that actively promote hiring individuals from marginalized communities and provide training and support to ensure their success within the organization. Additionally, measures can be taken to ensure that compensation and promotions are fair and based on merit, rather than biased norms.

Within the criminal justice system, equity and social justice considerations aim to address issues such as racial and socio-economic disparities in arrests, convictions, and sentencing. These considerations center around reducing systemic biases and ensuring that all individuals, regardless of their background, are treated fairly and justly.

For example, reforms may involve implementing training programs for law enforcement and legal professionals regarding implicit bias and promoting alternatives to incarceration for nonviolent offenses. Additionally, efforts may be made to increase community engagement and law enforcement transparency to improve trust between marginalized communities and the criminal justice system.

To conclude, equity and social justice considerations are vital in numerous aspects of society. They involve proactively addressing systemic inequalities and biases that persist in order to create a more inclusive and fair society. These considerations are essential to ensure that everyone, irrespective of their background, has access to equal opportunities, resources, and protections.

Chapter 13: International Politics, Policies, and Agreements

International politics play a crucial role in shaping global affairs and determining the relationships between nations. This chapter explores the complex dynamics of international politics, focusing on the policies and agreements that shape the interactions between countries.

One of the key aspects of international politics is the balance of power between nations. Throughout history, different countries have wielded varying levels of influence and played significant roles in shaping global politics. The balance of power is often a delicate equilibrium that is continuously evolving with changing global dynamics.

The concept of geopolitics, which considers the geographical location and resources of a country, further adds to the complexity of international politics. Countries with strategic geographical advantages often wield more power and are better equipped to negotiate favorable policies and agreements with other nations.

In order to manage international politics effectively, countries engage in the development and implementation of policies that guide their interactions with other nations. The policies of a country are influenced by a myriad of factors, including its domestic politics, national interests, and foreign policy objectives. These policies can range from economic and trade policies to security and defense policies.

International agreements play a vital role in shaping the relationships and interactions between nations. These agreements, often negotiated between countries, governmental organizations, or international bodies, provide a framework for cooperation, conflict resolution, and the establishment of new norms and regulations. International agreements cover a wide range of issues, including trade, environmental policies, human rights, and security.

One of the most prominent examples of international agreements is the United Nations (UN). Established in 1945, the UN is a multinational organization aimed at promoting peace, stability, and cooperation among its member states. Through the various branches such as the General Assembly, Security Council, and specialized agencies, the UN facilitates the negotiation of agreements that address a broad range of global challenges.

Global trade policies and agreements also play a significant role in shaping international politics. Organizations such as the World Trade Organization (WTO) ensure a framework for negotiating and implementing global trade agreements, reducing trade barriers, and resolving trade disputes. These policies impact countries' economies, influence their political relationships, and contribute to shaping the overall global economic landscape.

International politics also encompass regional dynamics and regional agreements. Regional organizations such as the European Union (EU), Association of Southeast Asian Nations (ASEAN), and African Union (AU) promote regional integration and cooperation. These regional agreements often contribute to the stability and development of member states while shaping their international relations.

The chapter further explores the role of non-state actors in international politics. Non-governmental organizations (NGOs), multinational corporations, and global civil society play an influential role in shaping international politics by advocating for specific policies, advancing human rights agendas, and influencing the decision-making processes of governments and international bodies.

In today's interconnected world, international politics, policies, and agreements are crucial for managing global challenges, resolving conflicts, and advancing collective interests. From negotiations on climate change to actions against terrorism, international cooperation is essential in addressing complex global issues.

Within this chapter, readers will gain a comprehensive understanding of the intricacies of international politics, delve into various policies and agreements that shape the interactions between nations, and critically analyze the challenges and opportunities presented by the global political arena. Overall, the chapter presents a valuable insight into the complex world of international politics while highlighting the significance of policies and agreements in shaping the future of global affairs.

13.1 United Nations Framework Convention on Climate Change

The United Nations Framework Convention on Climate Change (UNFCCC) is an international treaty founded in 1992 with the goal of addressing the global issue of climate change. Often referred to simply as the UNFCCC, this agreement has become the main international instrument for addressing climate change and setting the framework for international climate negotiations.

The UNFCCC was established in response to the growing concerns about the environmental, social, and economic consequences of human-induced climate change. Its ultimate objective is to stabilize greenhouse gas concentrations in the Earth's atmosphere at a level that would prevent dangerous interference with the climate system. To achieve this, the UNFCCC focuses on promoting various measures, such as reducing greenhouse gas emissions, adapting to the impacts of climate change, and supporting developing countries in their efforts to combat climate change.

Key Components of the UNFCCC:

1. The Convention: The primary body of the UNFCCC is the Convention itself. It outlines the objectives, guiding principles, and obligations of its signatories. The Convention emphasizes the importance of equity and common but differentiated responsibilities, recognizing that developed countries have historically contributed more to climate change and should take the lead in combating it.

2. Conference of the Parties (COP): The COP is the central decision-making body of the UNFCCC. It comprises representatives from all countries that have ratified the Convention. They convene annually to review the implementation of climate change commitments, negotiate and adopt new decisions, and set overall policy directions for addressing climate change.

3. Kyoto Protocol: The Kyoto Protocol is an international treaty under the UNFCCC, adopted in 1997 and enforced from 2005 to 2020. It established

legally binding emission reduction targets for developed countries, known as Annex I Parties, for the first commitment period (2008-2012). The protocol also introduced market mechanisms, such as emissions trading and Clean Development Mechanism (CDM), to facilitate cost-effective greenhouse gas reductions globally.

4. Paris Agreement: The Paris Agreement is the most significant landmark achievement under the UNFCCC. It was adopted in 2015 and entered into force in 2016. The Agreement aims to limit global warming to well below 2 degrees Celsius above pre-industrial levels, while pursuing efforts to keep it below 1.5 degrees Celsius. Unlike the Kyoto Protocol, the Paris Agreement involves voluntary and nationally determined contributions (NDCs) to reducing greenhouse gas emissions from both developed and developing countries.

5. Adaptation: Adaptation to the effects of climate change is a critical component of the UNFCCC. The convention recognizes the need to support developing countries, particularly the most vulnerable, in building resilience and adapting to the impacts of climate change. Numerous funds have been established under the convention to finance adaptation initiatives, capacity-building, and technology transfer to developing nations.

6. Financial Mechanisms: The UNFCCC oversees several financial mechanisms to support climate change actions in developing countries. The Global Environment Facility (GEF) is a multilateral fund that provides financial assistance for climate change initiatives. Additionally, the Green Climate Fund (GCF), established under the Paris Agreement, aims to support developing countries in their transition to low-carbon and climate-resilient economies.

The impacts of climate change are ever-growing, and the importance of concerted global efforts to combat it cannot be overstated. The UNFCCC provides a platform for countries to come together, negotiate, and address the complexities of this global challenge. Through its various components and ongoing negotiations, the UNFCCC seeks to resolve key issues, strengthen international cooperation, and promote sustainable development in the face of climate change.

13.2 Kyoto Protocol, Paris Agreement, and Beyond

The Kyoto Protocol, the Paris Agreement, and what lies beyond these international agreements are crucial components of global efforts to combat climate change. These ambitious undertakings hold the key to addressing the pressing issue of rising greenhouse gas emissions and securing a sustainable future for our planet. In this article, we will delve into the unique aspects, accomplishments, and future prospects of these transformative initiatives.

The Kyoto Protocol: Sparking Global Climate Action

The Kyoto Protocol, adopted in 1997, became the first comprehensive climate agreement aimed at reducing worldwide emissions. It set binding targets for developed countries to cut their greenhouse gas emissions collectively by 5.2% below 1990 levels during the period from 2008 to 2012. The protocol provided instruments such as carbon markets and emissions trading to incentivize emission reductions efficiently.

Initially, the Kyoto Protocol had an impressive participation rate, with most developed countries committing to its targets. However, the exclusions of major emitters, such as the United States, from its provisions significantly limited its effectiveness. Despite this setback, the protocol introduced crucial mechanisms to tackle climate change and laid the groundwork for future agreements.

The Paris Agreement: A New Era of Global Cooperation

Building upon the foundations set by the Kyoto Protocol, the Paris Agreement was established in 2015 to galvanize global efforts to limit global warming to well below 2 degrees Celsius above pre-industrial levels and to pursue efforts to limit the temperature increase to 1.5 degrees Celsius. The agreement emphasized the principle of collective responsibility, urging all countries to engage in emission reduction efforts while considering their unique national circumstances.

One of the standout accomplishments of the Paris Agreement was its ability to secure virtually universal participation. To date, 190 parties have ratified the agreement, signifying profound recognition of the need for decisive climate action. Moreover, the agreement encourages countries to regularly revise and enhance their national climate targets to continuously scale up their ambition over time.

Beyond the Paris Agreement: Heralding a Decade of Action

As we move beyond the Paris Agreement, we enter a new era characterized by heightened urgency and an increased need for decisive action. The Intergovernmental Panel on Climate Change (IPCC) warns that we have only a narrow window of opportunity to limit global warming to 1.5 degrees Celsius, beyond which the impacts of climate change will be increasingly severe.

To this end, the Conference of the Parties (COP) to the UN Framework Convention on Climate Change (UNFCCC) has been actively convening annually to facilitate global climate negotiations and chart the course for enhanced climate action. COP26, slated to take place in Glasgow in November 2021, will be crucial in determining the trajectory of global efforts and solidifying commitments made under the Paris Agreement.

Moreover, technological advancements and societal transformations offer new avenues for climate action. Developments in renewable energy, electric mobility, and nature-based solutions present opportunities to decarbonize our economies and transition toward sustainable development. Concurrently, climate consciousness is transcending national borders, with youth-led movements and massive public mobilizations demanding urgent action from governments and businesses alike.

In conclusion, the Kyoto Protocol, the Paris Agreement, and the ongoing global climate negotiations signify significant milestones in humanity's fight against climate change. While the Kyoto Protocol initiated international cooperation, the Paris Agreement ushered in a new era of collaboration and ambition. As we look beyond these agreements, the challenges of climate change require intensified efforts, strengthened global cooperation, and accelerated action. The journey to a sustainable future necessitates perseverance, innovation, and the unwavering dedication of all nations and individuals alike.

13.3 Assessing the Efficacy of Global Climate Governance

Assessing the efficacy of global climate governance is crucial in understanding the effectiveness of the strategies and policies implemented to address climate change at the global level. With the increasing urgency to combat climate change and reduce greenhouse gas emissions, it is essential to evaluate the progress and impact of global climate governance frameworks on mitigating climate change effects.

One way to assess the efficacy of global climate governance is through evaluating the targets and commitments set by international agreements. The most notable agreement is the Paris Agreement, which aims to limit global warming well below 2 degrees Celsius above pre-industrial levels and pursue efforts to limit the temperature increase to 1.5 degrees Celsius. Evaluating the progress in achieving these temperature targets can provide insights into the effectiveness of global climate governance.

Additionally, the implementation of policies and initiatives to reduce greenhouse gas emissions is a crucial factor in assessing the efficacy of global climate governance. Countries are expected to develop and implement NDCs (Nationally Determined Contributions) to outline their emission reduction targets and strategies. Effectively implementing these policies, along with monitoring and reporting processes, can indicate the strength of global climate governance in driving action and reducing emissions.

Furthermore, the financial and technological support provided to developing countries in their efforts to adapt to climate change and mitigate its effects is an essential aspect of global climate governance assessment. The provision of necessary resources, technology transfers, and capacity-building initiatives can significantly influence the efficacy of global governance frameworks in addressing climate change on a global scale.

In addition to tangible outcomes, evaluating the political will and cooperation among nations is crucial in assessing the efficacy of global climate governance. Addressing climate change requires collective action and collaboration among countries, and analyzing the level of commitment and cooperation shown by nations can provide insights into the effectiveness of global climate governance structures.

It is also important to consider the level of public and private engagement in climate action initiatives while assessing the efficacy of global climate governance. Mobilizing public opinion and encouraging private sector involvement can bolster efforts to combat climate change, and their active participation signifies the strength and effectiveness of global governance initiatives.

Furthermore, the monitoring and reporting mechanisms established by global climate governance frameworks play a critical role in assessing their efficacy. Regular review and assessment of progress can help identify gaps and challenges, including the ineffectiveness of certain policies or strategies, thereby informing future decision-making processes.

Ultimately, assessing the efficacy of global climate governance is a complex process involving multiple factors, including the achievement of targets, policy implementation, financial support, political commitment, public and private engagement, and monitoring mechanisms. Evaluating these aspects helps identify strengths and weaknesses in global climate governance frameworks, driving improvements and ensuring more effective strategies in addressing the pressing issue of climate change.

Chapter 14: Scientific Research Initiatives and Important Studies

Scientific research initiatives play a crucial role in advancing our knowledge and understanding of the world around us. They provide us with valuable insights into various fields of study and help shape policies and practices. In this chapter, we will explore some significant scientific research initiatives and highlight valuable studies that have contributed significantly to their respective fields.

One of the most well-known research initiatives is the Human Genome Project (HGP), which aimed to map and sequence the entire human genome. This ambitious project, launched in 1990, involved numerous researchers from around the world. It had a profound impact on our understanding of genetics and has paved the way for advancements in personalized medicine, gene therapy, and forensic science. The successful completion of the HGP in 2003 represents a milestone achievement in scientific research.

Another important research initiative is the Large Hadron Collider (LHC), located at the European Organization for Nuclear Research (CERN). The LHC is the world's most powerful particle accelerator and has been instrumental in fundamental particle physics research. The experiments conducted at the LHC, such as the discovery of the Higgs boson in 2012, have helped validate the predictions of the Standard Model of particle physics and provide valuable insights into the fundamental properties of matter and the universe.

In the field of astronomy, the Kepler mission stands out as a significant research endeavor. Launched by NASA in 2009, the Kepler spacecraft was designed to search for exoplanets, planets outside our solar system, by detecting tiny variations in the brightness of stars. The mission has been highly successful, discovering thousands of exoplanets, including ones in the habitable zone where liquid water could exist. Kepler has revolutionized our understanding of exoplanets and their distribution in the galaxy, bringing us closer to the possibility of finding extraterrestrial life.

Moving on to important studies, the Asch conformity experiments are classic studies in social psychology. Conducted by Solomon Asch in the 1950s, these experiments demonstrated the power of social influence and conformity. Participants in the experiments were shown lines of different lengths and asked to match them with a reference line. When confederates purposely gave incorrect answers, a significant number of participants conformed to the incorrect majority opinion. This study shed light on the mechanisms of social conformity, providing valuable insights into group dynamics and the influence of group norms on individual decision-making.

In the field of neuroscience, the study by Karl Lashley on cortical localization of memory is an influential work. Lashley conducted experiments on rats, surgically removing parts of their brains to observe the effects on learning and memory. Contrary to the prevailing belief at the time that memories were stored in specific brain areas, Lashley found that memory was distributed across the cortex. This study challenged the dominant theory of memory and paved the way for new research and understanding of how memory functions in the brain.

In the realm of environmental science, the Millennium Ecosystem Assessment (MA) stands as a notable example. Established by the United Nations in 2000, the MA aimed to assess the consequences of ecosystem changes for human well-being. It involved over 1,300 scientists and policymakers from around the world and provided a comprehensive analysis of the state of the world's ecosystems. The MA highlighted the importance of maintaining and restoring ecosystems and called for urgent action to address environmental degradation and safeguard human and ecological health.

In conclusion, scientific research initiatives and important studies shape our understanding of the world and contribute to various fields of study. From groundbreaking initiatives like the Human Genome Project and the Large Hadron Collider to influential studies such as the Asch conformity experiments and Lashley's work on memory, these endeavors provide us with invaluable knowledge and insights. By supporting and promoting scientific research, we can continue to make significant breakthroughs and advancements in various fields, ultimately improving our lives and the world we live in.

14.1 Prioritizing Research in Global Warming and Ocean Acidification

Research on global warming and ocean acidification are two pressing issues that need to be prioritized. These phenomena are intricately connected, with global warming leading to increased ocean temperatures and subsequent implications on marine ecosystems. Moreover, the rise in carbon dioxide (CO2) emissions has resulted in the acidification of oceans, posing a significant threat to marine life and biodiversity.

To effectively prioritize research in these areas, it is crucial to understand the magnitude of their consequences. Global warming has led to rising sea levels, increased frequency and intensity of extreme weather events, disruptions in ecosystem dynamics, and detrimental effects on human populations in coastal regions. Similarly, ocean acidification threatens the vitality of coral reefs, mollusks, and other shell-forming marine organisms. These impacts have far-reaching consequences not only for the environment but also for economies reliant on marine resources.

In order to effectively tackle these issues, a multidisciplinary and collaborative approach is necessary. This approach should involve researchers, government agencies, policymakers, and organizations working together to find sustainable solutions. Prioritizing research means allocating resources to initiatives that directly address these topics, fostering innovation, and engaging communities in the process.

One crucial area of research that requires prioritization is the study of mitigation strategies to combat global warming. This includes investigating alternative energy sources, exploring carbon capture and storage technologies, and identifying sustainable practices for industries and energy production. By investing in these areas, we can reduce greenhouse gas emissions and halt the progression of global warming.

In addition to mitigation, adaptation is essential. Research should focus on developing strategies to minimize the adverse effects of global warming and ocean acidification on vulnerable regions and communities. This may involve identifying resilient coastal infrastructure designs, implementing effective disaster management strategies, and supporting vulnerable communities in adapting to changing environmental conditions.

Particular attention should also be given to understanding the biological impacts of ocean acidification. Research in this area can help assess which marine species are most at risk and understand the potential cascading effects on marine food webs. By comprehending the various mechanisms and impacts of ocean acidification, scientists can better assist policymakers in developing targeted interventions and conservation efforts.

Furthermore, as global warming and ocean acidification are global challenges, international collaboration is crucial. Establishing research networks and sharing data across nations is vital to foster cooperation and the exchange of knowledge. This collaboration can enable researchers to pool resources, conduct large-scale studies, and develop comprehensive models to better predict and mitigate the impacts of global warming and ocean acidification.

Education and public outreach should also be prioritized to create public awareness and promote behavioral and policy changes. Communicating scientific findings effectively is vital to foster support for research initiatives and promote sustainable practices on a broader scale. Encouraging public engagement empowers communities to take ownership of the issues at hand and become advocates for change.

In conclusion, prioritizing research on global warming and ocean acidification is crucial given their significant and interconnected repercussions. By focusing on mitigation and adaptation strategies, understanding biological impacts, promoting international collaboration, and prioritizing education and public outreach, we can make meaningful progress towards mitigating the effects of these global challenges.

14.2 Investigating Potential Solutions and New Discoveries

In the world of science and research, investigating potential solutions and new discoveries is an essential and exciting process. It involves employing various techniques and methodologies to unravel complex problems and uncover groundbreaking information. This demanding task requires persistence, resources, and a deep commitment to scientific inquiry.

One of the key aspects of investigating potential solutions and new discoveries is the extensive research that goes into gathering background knowledge and understanding existing information. Scientists delve into academic papers, reports, and previous studies to gain insights and build upon the work of others. This thorough examination of existing knowledge forms the foundation for exploring new possibilities and challenges existing assumptions.

Once armed with substantial background information, scientists design and implement experiments to test hypotheses and gather empirical evidence. These experiments can range from controlled laboratory settings to field research conducted in real-world scenarios. They often involve rigorous methodologies and precise measurements to ensure the validity and reliability of the data collected. The careful execution of experiments is crucial for obtaining accurate results and confirming or debunking existing theories.

Interpreting and analyzing the data is another critical aspect of investigating potential solutions and new discoveries. Scientists employ statistical methods, data visualization techniques, and complex algorithms to extract meaning and patterns from the collected data. This step involves careful scrutiny and critical thinking to draw meaningful conclusions from often vast and intricate datasets. It is through this analytical process that scientists can identify potential solutions or make new discoveries that challenge prevailing scientific ideas.

Furthermore, communicating the findings to the scientific community and the public is paramount in the process of investigating potential solutions and new discoveries. Scientists publish their research in academic journals, deliver presentations at conferences, and engage in collaboration with peers to share their work and gather feedback. This information exchange allows for rigorous peer review, constructive criticism, and collaborative efforts towards fostering further advancements in the field.

Investigating potential solutions and new discoveries can lead to significant breakthroughs across a wide range of fields. It can pave the way for medical advances, technological innovations, and shifts in our understanding of the natural world. For example, exploring potential solutions to climate change can result in the development of renewable energy sources or advances in carbon sequestration technologies. Investigating new discoveries in medicine can lead to the development of life-saving drugs or therapies that revolutionize patient care.

In conclusion, investigating potential solutions and new discoveries is a complex and engaging process that plays a fundamental role in scientific advancement. It involves extensive background research, meticulous experimentation, careful data analysis, and effective communication. The pursuit of new knowledge and solutions is a continuous effort, driven by curiosity, collaboration, and a commitment to furthering our understanding of the world around us.

14.3 Collaborative Efforts among Scientists and Organizations

Collaboration among scientists and organizations plays a crucial role in advancing scientific research and overcoming complex challenges. In an era defined by rapid advancements in technology and a globalized world, collaborative efforts have become more essential than ever.

One of the key reasons why collaboration is so important is the complexity of scientific problems. Many scientific challenges require a multidisciplinary approach, combining the expertise of scientists from various fields. For example, tackling climate change requires input from climate scientists, ecologists, engineers, and economists, among others. By bringing together scientists from different disciplines, organizations can foster innovative solutions that are more holistic and effective.

Collaborative efforts also allow for the sharing of resources, knowledge, and expertise. Scientists and organizations often work in silos, typically with limited access to specialized equipment and facilities. Collaboration provides an opportunity to pool resources and access specialized tools that may not be available to individual scientists. This sharing of resources can dramatically accelerate research and enhance its impact.

Additionally, collaboration facilitates the sharing of knowledge and expertise. Scientists often work in their respective fields and are focused on their own research projects. However, through collaboration, they can exchange ideas, learn from one another, and build upon each other's work. This can lead to breakthroughs and accelerated progress in scientific discoveries. Collaborative efforts also allow scientists to explore research topics that are beyond their domain expertise, sparking novel ideas and innovations.

Another benefit of collaboration is the opportunity to leverage diverse perspectives. Scientists from different backgrounds bring unique viewpoints shaped by their personal experiences and cultural context. By embracing diversity within collaborative efforts, organizations promote a more inclusive and comprehensive understanding of scientific problems. This not only enhances the quality of research but also fosters inclusivity in scientific communities.

Moreover, collaboration extends beyond the scientific community. In many cases, addressing pressing environmental, social, and health challenges requires collaboration with policymakers, government agencies, non-governmental organizations, and industry. These stakeholders possess invaluable insights, resources, and networks that can significantly impact research outcomes and policy development. By involving multiple stakeholders in the collaborative process, scientists and organizations increase the likelihood of having tangible impact and developing workable solutions.

In recent years, technology has provided new possibilities for collaboration among scientists and organizations. Virtual collaboration tools, such as video conferencing and shared workspaces, enable scientists from different parts of the world to connect, exchange ideas, and work together on common projects. Platforms designed to foster collaboration, such as research networks and open-access journals, can facilitate the sharing of knowledge and resources at an unprecedented scale. These technological advancements have the potential to revolutionize the way scientists and organizations collaborate, making it easier, faster, and more accessible.

In conclusion, collaborative efforts among scientists and organizations are fundamental to the advancement of scientific research. Collaboration allows for the integration of diverse expertise, pooling of resources, sharing of knowledge, and leveraging diverse perspectives. The complexity of modern scientific problems and the interconnected nature of global challenges make collaborative efforts essential for scientific progress. As technology continues to evolve, so too will the opportunities and possibilities for collaborative endeavors, paving the way for breakthroughs and transformative discoveries.

Chapter 15: Case Studies: Local and Global Efforts in Combating Global Warming and Ocean Acidification

In Chapter 15, we delve into the fascinating world of case studies examining local and global efforts in combating global warming and ocean acidification. This chapter provides extensive and captivating information, shedding light on the various initiatives and strategies undertaken by individuals, communities, and governments to address these pressing environmental challenges.

Firstly, the chapter explores the case study of a small coastal town in the United States that has taken remarkable steps to combat global warming. Through a series of comprehensive actions such as transitioning to renewable energy sources, implementing sustainable waste management practices, and promoting green transportation options, this town has achieved substantial reductions in its carbon footprint. Furthermore, the case study delves into how the local government and community have come together to raise awareness about the importance of environmental sustainability and inspire other towns to follow in their footsteps.

Moving on to the global scale, the chapter presents a case study that examines international efforts to combat ocean acidification. It delves into the global network of scientists, policymakers, and environmental organizations who are collaborating to understand and mitigate the impacts of ocean acidification. From monitoring and studying the effects of acidification on marine ecosystems to promoting policy changes and sustainable fishing practices, this case study illuminates the immense collective effort being made worldwide to protect our precious oceans.

Moreover, the chapter delves into the case study of a developing nation that has made significant strides in combating global warming. It highlights the innovative policies and practices this nation has implemented, including afforestation programs, renewable energy investments, and sustainable agricultural practices. The case study not only underscores that even countries with limited resources can participate in the fight against global warming but also demonstrates that their efforts can yield significant positive impacts on a global scale.

Additionally, the chapter presents a case study on a multinational corporation that has taken extensive measures to reduce its carbon footprint. It examines the company's efforts to transition towards renewable energy sources, optimize energy efficiency, and adopt sustainable production and distribution practices. The case study highlights the far-reaching influence that large corporations can have on global emissions reduction and the importance of corporate social responsibility in addressing climate change.

Overall, Chapter 15 provides an in-depth analysis of a diverse range of case studies on local and global efforts in combating global warming and ocean acidification. It offers a wealth of detailed information that not only informs readers about the challenges at hand but also inspires and empowers them to take action in their own communities. The combination of comprehensive details and engaging narratives makes this chapter a captivating read for anyone interested in understanding current efforts to combat these pressing environmental issues.

15.1 Success Stories from Around the World

Success stories serve as powerful motivators, inspiring individuals from all walks of life to strive for greatness. This compilation highlights 15.1 remarkable success stories from diverse corners of the world, showcasing the triumph of willpower, determination, and talent that can overcome the odds. Each story demonstrates the incredible feats accomplished by ordinary people who refused to be limited by their circumstances, inspiring generations to dream big and achieve even bigger.

1. Malala Yousafzai- Pakistan:

Malala Yousafzai, a young Pakistani education activist, survived an assassination attempt by the Taliban and didn't let it deter her mission for girls' education. She went on to become the youngest person to receive the Nobel Peace Prize and has become a global voice for advocating girls' rights and quality education.

2. Elon Musk- South Africa:

Born in South Africa, Elon Musk is now a prominent entrepreneur and visionary leading the way in technological advancement. His remarkable success includes co-founding PayPal, Tesla Motors, SpaceX, and SolarCity, all revolutionary investments within their respective fields.

3. Oprah Winfrey- United States:

Oprah Winfrey, hailing from an impoverished background in the United States, overcame numerous obstacles to become a household name. She transformed herself from a local news anchor to a globally recognized television personality, philanthropist, and successful media executive.

4. Jack Ma- China:

Jack Ma, the founder of Alibaba Group, emerged from humble beginnings in China. Despite multiple rejections, he persisted with his e-commerce platform and eventually built it into one of the largest global companies, revolutionizing the entire online marketplace.

5. Li Ka-shing- Hong Kong:

Nicknamed the "Superman of Asia," Li Ka-shing progressed from poverty in war-torn China to achieving unrivaled entrepreneurial success. He built a global business empire, spanning sectors such as real estate, ports, telecommunications, and energy, making him Hong Kong's wealthiest man.

6. J.K. Rowling- United Kingdom:

Facing financial struggles and depression, J.K. Rowling wrote the iconic Harry Potter series, which went on to captivate millions worldwide. The immense success of her novels and subsequent film adaptations made her one of the best-selling authors in history.

7. Aliko Dangote- Nigeria:

Hailing from an African country grappling with economic challenges, Aliko Dangote became Africa's richest person with his business ventures in cement, commodities, and telecommunications. He showcases the potential for African entrepreneurs to impact substantial economic growth.

8. Nelson Mandela- South Africa:

Nelson Mandela, an icon of peace and resilience, transformed from a political prisoner to South Africa's first black President. Through his perseverance and visionary leadership, he contributed to dismantling apartheid and inspiring global change.

9. Serena Williams- United States:

Serena Williams, an African-American woman, conquered the sport of tennis, setting new standards of athleticism, power, and grace. Despite facing discrimination and adversity, she became one of the most dominant and celebrated athletes of all time.

10. Lise Meitner- Austria:

Lise Meitner, a Jewish-Austrian physicist, overcame gender and religious bias to play a pivotal role in discovering nuclear fission. Her groundbreaking work laid the foundation for modern nuclear physics and the unlocking of immense energy potential.

11. Stephen Hawking- United Kingdom:

Living with a debilitating motor neuron disease, Stephen Hawking emerged as one of the greatest theoretical physicists of our time. His contributions to our understanding of black holes and the nature of the universe revolutionized the field of cosmology.

12. Sir Richard Branson- United Kingdom:

With sheer determination and an entrepreneurial spirit, Sir Richard Branson built the Virgin Group, a conglomerate encompassing various industries such as music, airlines, and telecommunications. His leadership and philanthropic pursuits have left an indelible mark on society.

13. Dr. Sanduk Ruit- Nepal:

Dr. Sanduk Ruit, an eye surgeon from Nepal, revolutionized cataract treatment, enabling thousands of impoverished individuals to regain their sight. His low-cost surgical technique has become a global standard, transforming the lives of millions across the developing world.

14. Ratan Tata- India:

Ratan Tata, an Indian industrialist and philanthropist, led the Tata Group to unprecedented growth and transformation. Under his leadership, Tata Motors acquired Jaguar Land Rover, solidifying its global presence in the automotive industry.

15. Esther Mahlangu- South Africa:

Esther Mahlangu, a renowned South African artist, promoted traditional Ndebele culture through her striking contemporary art. Despite limited education and resources, her intricate paintings adorn walls globally, celebrating African heritage and raising awareness.

THESE SUCCESS STORIES inspire us to dream, persist, and conquer despite obstacles. From entrepreneurs reshaping industries to activists fighting for justice, the triumphs of these individuals demonstrate the boundless potential within every human. As we embrace their stories and strive to emulate their audacity, we empower ourselves and shape a future where determination prevails and dreams become reality.

15.2 Key Lessons Learned and Best Practices

In this section, we will delve into the essential lessons and best practices that have been learned over the years. These insights have helped organizations and individuals navigate challenges and achieve greater success. By implementing these key lessons, you can enhance your decision-making ability and optimize your approach to various tasks. Let's explore these impactful insights and gain valuable knowledge.

1.Best Practices in Project Management:

- Define clear project objectives: Before initiating any project, it is critical to establish succinct and measurable objectives. This assists in keeping the team focused and aligned towards a tangible outcome.

- Effective communication: Maintain open lines of communication with all stakeholders. This ensures everyone is updated on project status, possible challenges, and expectations, fostering a collaborative working environment.

- Proactive risk assessment: Identify potential project risks as early as possible and develop contingency plans. Regular risk assessments allow for effective mitigation strategies and minimize future disruptions.

2. Strategies for Successful Negotiations:

- Prepare thoroughly: Adequate research about the negotiating party, market conditions, and potential alternatives is essential. This preparation enables you to approach negotiations from a position of strength.

- Aim for a win-win outcome: Strive to find mutually beneficial solutions by exploring areas where both parties can gain. This approach fosters long-term relationships and future collaborations.

- Active listening: Give full attention to the other party's perspective by actively listening. This not only helps you understand their underlying concerns but also establishes rapport and trust.

3. Lessons in Leadership and Team Management:

- Lead by example: Exhibit the values and behaviors you expect from your team. When leaders demonstrate dedication, professionalism, and empathy, it sets a positive precedent for the entire group.

- Encourage continuous learning: Encourage team members to upskill and learn from one another. Foster a culture of knowledge-sharing and provide resources and opportunities for personal and professional growth.

- Foster a healthy work-life balance: Understand the importance of mental and physical well-being. Promote an environment that values work-life balance and provide support systems to maintain employee engagement and overall satisfaction.

4. Effective Marketing and Communication:

- Tailor messages to target audiences: Understanding your audience and employing the appropriate communication channels and language strengthens the impact of your marketing efforts.

- Consistent branding: Maintain consistency across all marketing platforms to create a recognizable and cohesive brand identity. This builds trust and establishes a strong presence in the marketplace.

- Utilize analytics and feedback: Leverage data analytics and user feedback to measure the effectiveness of marketing campaigns. This information enables informed decision-making and aids in refining strategies.

THE 15.2 KEY LESSONS learned and best practices covered in this section serve as valuable guidelines for organizations and individuals looking to achieve excellence. By implementing these insights, you can strengthen your project management skills, negotiation tactics, leadership abilities, and marketing strategies. Embracing continuous learning and improvement will ensure longevity and success in any endeavor.

15.3 Inspiring Individuals and Grassroots Movements

In this chapter, we will explore the stories of 15.3 inspiring individuals and grassroots movements that have left a lasting impact on society. From those who fought for civil rights to the environmentalists who worked tirelessly to protect our planet, these individuals and groups have shown that a single person or a small community can make a significant difference.

One such individual is Rosa Parks. Born on February 4, 1913, in Tuskegee, Alabama, Parks became an instrumental figure in the American Civil Rights Movement. On December 1, 1955, she famously refused to give up her seat on a bus to a white passenger in Montgomery, Alabama. Her act of defiance sparked the Montgomery Bus Boycott, a year-long campaign that aimed to end racial segregation on public buses. Through her courage and determination, Parks became a symbol of resistance against racial injustice and inspired countless others to join the fight for equality.

Another inspiring figure is Mahatma Gandhi, the leader of the Indian independence movement against British rule. Gandhi firmly believed in nonviolent resistance and civil disobedience to achieve political and social change. His philosophy of Satyagraha, or the pursuit of truth and nonviolence, influenced movements around the world. Under his guidance, millions of Indians participated in acts of nonviolent protest that eventually led to India's independence in 1947. Gandhi's legacy continues to inspire people of all backgrounds to stand up against injustice and work towards a more peaceful and just society.

In addition to individuals, grassroots movements have proven to be powerful catalysts for change. Take Greenpeace, for instance. Founded in 1971 by a small group of activists, this organization has become a global powerhouse in advocating for environmental protection. Its campaigns and direct actions have brought attention to critical issues such as climate change, deforestation, and endangered species preservation. Greenpeace's commitment to peaceful protests and grassroots organizing has spurred governments and corporations to address environmental issues and adopt more sustainable practices.

In a similar vein, the Occupy Wall Street movement gained international attention in 2011 with its powerful message against economic inequality and corporate greed. What began as a small group of activists camping out in Zuccotti Park in New York City quickly grew into a global movement. Protesters held demonstrations, organized sit-ins, and used social media to raise awareness about the growing wealth divide. Although the movement faced criticism and ultimately disbanded, it succeeded in raising public consciousness about economic disparities and starting a vital dialogue about the need for systemic change.

These are just four examples of the many inspiring individuals and movements that have shaped our world. From Spartacus leading a slave rebellion in ancient Rome to Malala Yousafzai advocating for girls' education today, their stories serve as beacons of hope and remind us of the power that lies within each of us to effect change. Whether it is championing human rights, fighting for social justice, or protecting the environment, these individuals and grassroots movements have shown us that ordinary people can do extraordinary things. Ultimately, their stories serve as an inspiration for all of us to stand up for what we believe in and work towards a better future for everyone.

Chapter 16: Ethical Considerations and Responsibilities

In today's rapidly evolving world, where technological advancements and globalization have interconnected us like never before, it becomes crucial to recognize and address the ethical considerations and responsibilities faced by individuals, organizations, and societies. The realm of ethics encompasses a wide range of moral principles and values that guide human behavior, decision-making, and accountability.

One of the fundamental ethical considerations is the responsibility to respect the dignity and rights of all human beings. This includes treating others with fairness, justice, and equality, regardless of their race, gender, ethnicity, or socio-economic status. In the business world, this means promoting diversity and inclusion, providing equal employment opportunities, and eliminating discrimination in any form.

Ethical responsibilities also extend to environmental considerations and sustainability. With the escalating issues of climate change and depletion of natural resources, individuals and organizations are obliged to minimize their impact on the environment. This involves adopting sustainable practices, such as reducing carbon emissions, conserving energy, and managing waste responsibly. By doing so, we ensure a better future for generations to come.

Moreover, ethical considerations arise in the realm of data privacy and cybersecurity. In today's data-driven age, where personal and sensitive information is constantly being collected and shared, it becomes crucial to uphold individuals' privacy rights and protect their data from unauthorized access. As individuals entrusted with such information, organizations must implement robust security measures and ensure compliance with data protection regulations to maintain the trust and confidence of their stakeholders.

Another critical ethical consideration revolves around transparency and honesty in communication. In both personal and professional settings, individuals and organizations are expected to be truthful and disclose relevant information, eschewing deceit or intentional misrepresentation. Transparency promotes trust, credibility, and fosters authentic relationships, which are vital for both personal well-being and organizational success.

Ethical responsibilities also pertain to responsibilities towards future generations and social welfare. This means acknowledging the impact of our actions and decisions on the well-being and lives of future generations. Organizations should adopt long-term, sustainable strategies that take into account the interests of subsequent generations. Additionally, engaging in philanthropic activities and giving back to society helps address social issues and disparities, contributing towards an equitable and more compassionate world.

In conclusion, ethical considerations and responsibilities play a crucial role in guiding our behavior, decisions, and interactions with others, as well as shaping the world we live in. By embracing a sense of ethical duty, respect for human rights, environmental sustainability, personal privacy, transparency, and social welfare, we can collectively work towards creating a more just, equitable, and ethically responsible society. Ethics must be an integral part of our daily lives and should be prioritized in all aspects of decision-making Processes.

16.1 Ethical Frameworks for Addressing Climate Change

Climate change poses one of the greatest threats to human well-being and the environment. As such, it raises several ethical questions that need to be addressed. In response, various ethical frameworks have been developed to guide decision-making and action in tackling climate change. These frameworks attempt to balance the interests of present and future generations, as well as the rights and responsibilities of individuals and governments.

One commonly used ethical framework is the utilitarian approach. Utilitarianism focuses on maximizing overall happiness and minimizing overall suffering. In the context of climate change, this approach argues that actions should be taken to minimize the negative impacts on both present and future generations. For example, policies might be implemented to reduce greenhouse gas emissions and transition to clean and renewable energy sources.

Another ethical framework is the rights-based approach. According to this perspective, all individuals have certain inherent rights that should be respected. In the context of climate change, this would entail recognizing the rights of those affected by its consequences. For instance, people vulnerable to the impacts of climate change, such as populations in low-lying coastal areas, have the right to be protected from its consequences and to have their voices heard in decision-making processes.

The justice-based approach is also relevant to addressing climate change. This framework focuses on distributive justice, which involves the fair distribution of resources and burdens. In the context of climate change, it recognizes that some regions and populations will be more heavily affected than others. This approach calls for measures that address these inequalities and ensure that the costs and benefits of climate action are divided fairly.

A fourth ethical framework is the precautionary principle. This principle suggests taking preventive action in the face of uncertainty. When it comes to climate change, this would mean adopting measures to reduce greenhouse gas emissions even if the scientific evidence is not conclusive. It emphasizes the importance of erring on the side of caution when dealing with risks that could have catastrophic consequences.

In addition to these ethical frameworks, several subsidiary norms and principles exist. For example, intergenerational equity emphasizes the responsibility of current generations to ensure a sustainable and livable environment for future generations. Public engagement and inclusion emphasize the importance of involving diverse stakeholders in decision-making processes to ensure better outcomes and representation of all interests.

Overall, the ethical frameworks for addressing climate change provide guidance for decision-making and action. By balancing the considerations of utility, rights, justice, and precaution, these frameworks strive to foster solutions that address the urgent challenges posed by climate change while also maintaining fairness, equity, and sustainability. As the climate crisis intensifies, it becomes increasingly important to fully understand and apply these frameworks in order to forge a path towards a more climate-resilient and ethically responsible future.

16.2 Different Perspectives on Responsibility

When it comes to responsibility, there are many different perspectives to consider. People have varying beliefs and opinions about what it means to be responsible, as well as how responsibility should be assigned and upheld in different contexts. In this article, we will explore 16.2 different perspectives on responsibility.

1. Individual Responsibility: This perspective emphasizes that responsibility is primarily an individual duty. Each person bears the responsibility for their own actions, choices, and consequences. This viewpoint places a heavy emphasis on personal accountability.

2. Collective Responsibility: Contrasting the individual perspective, collective responsibility holds that responsibility can and should be shared among group members. It emphasizes the idea that we are all interconnected and that the actions of one can impact the entire group.

3. Moral Responsibility: From a moral standpoint, responsibility refers to the obligation to act in accordance with ethical principles and values. Individuals are considered morally responsible for their actions and can be held accountable for any harm they cause.

4. Legal Responsibility: This perspective focuses on responsibility as defined by laws and regulations. Legal responsibility determines what actions are considered acceptable or unacceptable within a particular legal framework and outlines the consequences for violations.

5. Social Responsibility: This viewpoint places emphasis on the responsibility individuals or organizations have towards society as a whole. Socially responsible actions are those that promote the well-being and welfare of others, such as engaging in philanthropy or sustainable business practices.

6. Environmental Responsibility: Similarly, environmental responsibility is concerned with the duty to protect and preserve the natural world. It involves actions that promote sustainability, conservation, and mitigate or prevent harm to the environment.

7. Parental Responsibility: Parents have a unique responsibility to care for and nurture their children. This perspective emphasizes the duties and obligations parents have towards their offspring, including providing for their physical, emotional, and psychological needs.

8. Corporate Responsibility: In the realm of business, corporate responsibility refers to the obligation of companies to act in a socially and environmentally responsible manner. This can involve initiatives such as fair labor practices, ethical sourcing, and transparency.

9. Professional Responsibility: This perspective centers around the responsibilities individuals have within their specific professions. Professionals are expected to adhere to certain ethical standards and conduct themselves in a way that ensures the well-being and best interests of their clients or patients.

10. Political Responsibility: Political actors, such as elected officials or public servants, have a responsibility to represent and serve the public interest. This perspective emphasizes the need for accountability and transparency in governance.

11. Economic Responsibility: Economic responsibility focuses on the duty of individuals, organizations, and governments to promote economic stability and growth. It involves managing resources wisely, minimizing waste, and contributing to economic development.

12. Cultural Responsibility: Cultural responsibility highlights the obligation individuals have to respect and preserve their own cultural heritage while also respecting the diversity of other cultures. It promotes understanding, tolerance, and inclusivity.

13. Gender Responsibility: This perspective addresses the need for gender equality and the sharing of responsibilities between genders. It calls for the recognition and elimination of gender disparities, stereotypes, and discrimination.

14. Intergenerational Responsibility: As stewards of the Earth, there is a responsibility towards future generations to preserve and improve the world in which they will live. This perspective emphasizes sustainability and leaving a positive legacy.

15. Emotional Responsibility: Emotional responsibility refers to the duty individuals have to manage and regulate their emotions in a healthy and

constructive manner. This includes taking ownership of one's emotions and ensuring they do not negatively impact oneself or others.

16. Self-Responsibility: Lastly, self-responsibility centers on the idea that individuals have the power and autonomy to take charge of their own lives. It emphasizes personal growth, self-care, and self-improvement.

These are just 16.2 of the many different perspectives on responsibility. Each offers unique insights into what it means to be responsible and how responsibility should be understood and applied in various domains. Understanding these perspectives can help us navigate complex ethical, social, and personal dilemmas and make informed decisions that uphold accountability and promote well-being.

16.3 Moral Imperatives for Future Generations

One of the most prominent moral imperatives for future generations is that of sustainability. As the global population continues to grow, the demand for resources increases exponentially. It is essential that we prioritize the sustainable use of these resources to ensure a more equitable distribution and prevent future generations from facing resource scarcity and environmental degradation.

Another vital moral imperative for future generations is social justice. We must work to create a society where everyone has equal access to basic necessities such as food, healthcare, education, and clean water. This includes rectifying the existing social inequalities and injustices that persist today. By addressing issues such as poverty, discrimination, and inequality, we can create a more just and equitable world for future generations.

Furthermore, a moral imperative for future generations is intergenerational solidarity. This concept recognizes that our actions today will have significant consequences for future generations, making it imperative to consider long-term effects rather than focusing solely on short-term gains. By practicing intergenerational solidarity, we can ensure that the decisions we make reflect a sense of responsibility and consideration for the needs and well-being of those who come after us.

Moral imperatives for future generations also revolve around environmental stewardship. Humans have had a significant impact on the planet, resulting in climate change, deforestation, and habitat loss. We must understand that we share this planet with countless other species, and it is our duty to act as responsible stewards of the Earth. By preserving and restoring ecosystems, as well as promoting sustainable practices, we can mitigate the adverse effects of climate change and protect biodiversity for future generations to enjoy.

Furthermore, it is crucial to consider the moral imperative of technological advancement. Technology has transformed the world in countless ways, improving the quality of life for many. However, we must also recognize that technology can have negative consequences, such as job displacement and privacy concerns. It is our moral duty to navigate technological advancements ethically, ensuring that they benefit society as a whole and do not result in harm or inequality for future generations.

In summary, encompass a range of principles aimed at creating a sustainable, just, and equitable world for those yet to come. It is our responsibility to prioritize sustainability, social justice, intergenerational solidarity, environmental stewardship, and ethical technological advancements. By adhering to these imperatives, we can leave a positive and lasting impact on the world for future generations.

Chapter 17: Conclusion - Charting a Sustainable Future

In this final chapter, we summarize the key insights and recommendations presented throughout this book and discuss their implications for charting a sustainable future. We have explored a wide range of topics related to sustainability, encompassing economic, social, and environmental dimensions. Through this exploration, we have sought to shed light on the interconnectedness and complexity of these issues, as well as the urgent need for collective action.

One of the primary insights that emerges from our analysis is the recognition that sustainability is not just an option or a luxury; it is a necessity. Our current mode of development is plagued by environmental degradation, social inequality, and economic instability. We cannot sustain this trajectory without compromising the well-being of present and future generations. Therefore, it is vital that we shift towards a more sustainable path, one that balances the needs of people, planet, and economy.

This shift requires a transformation across all sectors of society. In the economic realm, we need to move away from a growth-at-all-costs paradigm and embrace a more inclusive and circular economy. A circular economy aims to minimize waste and maximize resource efficiency, while also promoting social well-being and equitable distribution of wealth. It is a model that prioritizes sustainable production and consumption practices, fostering innovation and value creation without depleting natural resources.

The social dimension of sustainability also demands attention. We must address the deep-rooted inequalities that exist within and across societies. Poverty eradication, access to quality education, healthcare, and clean water are fundamental rights that must be safeguarded for all. Moreover, promoting gender equality and social inclusion is essential for building resilient and sustainable communities. Embracing diversity and ensuring equitable opportunities for all is not only morally right but also economically beneficial, as it fosters innovation and enhances social cohesion.

From an environmental standpoint, it is crucial to recognize the finite nature of our planet's resources and the urgent need for planetary stewardship. Climate change, biodiversity loss, and pollution are threatening our very existence. We must transition towards renewable energy sources, reduce our reliance on fossil fuels, and invest in sustainable technologies. Carbon neutrality must be achieved, emissions must be reduced, and nature must be conserved and restored. The transition to a sustainable future requires concerted efforts at both the individual and collective levels.

To achieve these ambitious goals, we need effective governance systems and international cooperation. Governments, businesses, civil society, and individuals all play a role in shaping our collective future. Institutional reforms, transparent decision-making processes, and inclusive policy frameworks are essential in uniting diverse stakeholders towards a common vision. Collaborative actions and partnerships are necessary for addressing global challenges that transcend national borders and require coordinated efforts.

In conclusion, charting a sustainable future requires a fundamental shift in our values, behaviors, and decision-making processes. Sustainability should no longer be a buzzword; it must guide our actions and permeate all aspects of society. The insights and recommendations presented in this book offer pathways for achieving a more sustainable future. It is now up to us to take charge and create the world we want to live in, one that operates within the planetary boundaries while ensuring well-being and prosperity for all. Let us embark on this transformative journey together, for the sake of current and future generations.

17.1 Recapitulation of the Global Warming-Ocean Acidification Linkage

In order to fully understand the connection between global warming and ocean acidification, it is crucial to recapitulate the various aspects of this complex linkage. Global warming refers to the long-term increase in average temperature of Earth's atmosphere, primarily caused by the release of greenhouse gases (GHGs) from human activities such as burning fossil fuels, deforestation, and industrial processes. On the other hand, ocean acidification refers to the ongoing decrease in the pH of seawater as a result of increased carbon dioxide (CO_2) levels in the atmosphere. While these two phenomena are distinct, they are intricately linked and share common causative agents.

To comprehend the linkage between global warming and ocean acidification, it is important to delve into the carbon cycle. The natural carbon cycle involves the exchange of carbon between the atmosphere, oceans, biosphere, and geosphere. Oceans are among the largest carbon sinks on Earth and currently play a vital role in absorbing around 30% of human-released CO_2. However, the massive influx of CO_2 from burning fossil fuels disrupts this balance, leading to a surplus accumulation of carbon in the oceans.

As CO_2 dissolves in seawater, it reacts with water molecules to form carbonic acid—a process known as ocean acidification. This reaction causes a decrease in seawater pH and alters the carbonate chemistry of the ocean. The carbonate ion concentration decreases, making it harder for species like corals, mollusks, and shellfish to produce and maintain their calcium carbonate shells and structures. This puts these organisms at risk as their ability to survive and reproduce is compromised. Moreover, a lower pH also negatively affects marine organisms at earlier stages of development such as the larvae of fish and crustaceans.

The connection with global warming becomes evident when considering the main driver of oceanic CO_2 uptake: increased atmospheric carbon dioxide. The same human activities that are responsible for rising temperatures in the atmosphere also lead to higher levels of CO2 in the air, which in turn leads to elevated carbon dioxide absorption by the oceans. This mutual relationship further exacerbates global climate change as more atmospheric CO2 enters the ocean, resulting in increased ocean acidification, and subsequently increasing the negative impacts on marine ecosystems.

The consequences of this global warming-ocean acidification linkage are wide-ranging and worrisome. Not only do they threaten the stability of marine ecosystems and biodiversity, but they also have severe economic consequences for industries dependent on the health of oceans, such as fisheries and tourism. Additionally, the effect on marine life influences the food web and ecosystems as a whole, potentially leading to cascading effects throughout the entire biosphere.

Efforts to mitigate global warming and ocean acidification must, therefore, address both issues simultaneously. Reducing GHG emissions through clean energy technologies and sustainable practices is crucial to curbing global warming. Additionally, measures need to be taken to promote the resilience of marine ecosystems, such as the protection and restoration of critical habitats like coral reefs and seagrass meadows.

In conclusion, the linkage between global warming and ocean acidification is rooted in the excessive release of CO2 into the atmosphere by human activities. The resulting increase in atmospheric carbon dioxide disrupts the natural carbon cycle, leading to elevated CO2 absorption and subsequent acidification of the oceans. This connection carries significant consequences for marine life, ecosystems, and the overall health of our planet. Addressing this linkage necessitates reducing greenhouse gas emissions and implementing sustainable practices to ensure the protection and resilience of marine ecosystems.

17.2 Encouraging Solutions for Global Warming

Global warming, an issue that has gained increasing attention over the past few decades, poses a significant threat to our planet's environment and ecosystems. The escalating levels of greenhouse gases, primarily carbon dioxide emitted from human activities, have resulted in rising global temperatures, altered weather patterns, and an array of detrimental consequences. The urgency to tackle global warming has prompted scientists, policymakers, and individuals worldwide to search for viable solutions that can mitigate this global crisis.

One encouraging solution to combat global warming lies in the rapid transition from fossil fuels to renewable energy sources. Renewable energy, such as solar power, wind energy, and hydropower, generates electricity without emitting carbon dioxide or significant pollutants. Encouragingly, the cost of renewable energy technologies has significantly decreased over the past decade, making them more affordable and widely accessible. This switch not only reduces greenhouse gas emissions but also promotes energy independence and creates job opportunities in the rapidly growing renewable energy sector.

Furthermore, energy efficiency measures play a vital role in addressing global warming. Implementing energy-efficient technologies, practices, and behavior changes can substantially reduce energy consumption, consequently lowering greenhouse gas emissions. Energy-efficient buildings, appliances, and transportation systems conserve resources, save money, and reduce carbon footprints. Innovative strategies, such as smart grids, bioenergy, and recycling waste heat, contribute to boosting overall energy efficiency, making them crucial components in mitigating global warming.

Another noteworthy solution to tackle global warming is through reforestation and afforestation initiatives. Forests act as natural carbon sinks, absorbing carbon dioxide from the atmosphere through photosynthesis. However, rampant deforestation and habitat destruction have significantly reduced the Earth's capacity to absorb these emissions. Investing in forest conservation efforts, as well as promoting afforestation (the establishment of forests on previously non-forest land) and reforestation (reestablishment of forests on previously forested areas), can provide long-term benefits in combating global warming. This approach not only helps reduce carbon dioxide levels but also helps preserve biodiversity and promote sustainable land use practices.

In addition to these technological and ecological solutions, changes in individuals' everyday actions are essential to address global warming. Encouraging sustainable lifestyles through awareness campaigns and education can significantly reduce carbon footprints. Simple actions, such as conserving energy and water, reducing waste, adopting eco-friendly transportation methods, and supporting local and organic products, can collectively make a substantial positive impact on the environment. Moreover, initiatives that encourage the decentralization of food systems, such as promoting urban agriculture and reducing food waste, contribute to mitigating greenhouse gas emissions associated with food production and transportation.

Furthermore, international cooperation and policy frameworks are crucial to encourage solutions for global warming. The Paris Agreement, a global climate accord signed by nearly every nation, aims to limit global temperature rise by reducing greenhouse gas emissions and promoting sustainable development. International collaboration allows for knowledge sharing, technology transfer, and financial support to assist developing countries in adopting cleaner and more sustainable practices.

To conclude, addressing global warming necessitates a multifaceted approach involving technological advancements, ecological initiatives, individual actions, and international cooperation. Encouraging the transition to renewable energy, implementing energy-efficient measures, investing in reforestation, promoting sustainable lifestyles, and fostering international alliances are instrumental in combating global warming's adverse effects. It is imperative for each of us, as global citizens, to actively participate in and support these solutions, as they hold the key to a sustainable and healthier future for our planet.

17.3 Embracing the Urgency for Pathways to a Sustainable World

In recent decades, the issue of sustainability has gained increased attention and urgency. As the world grapples with various environmental challenges such as climate change, deforestation, overfishing, and depletion of natural resources, it has become clear that something needs to change in order to ensure a livable future for generations to come.

The urgency for pathways to a sustainable world lies in the fact that our current way of life is simply not sustainable in the long run. The Earth's resources are finite, and if we continue to extract them at the current rate, we will soon face severe shortages. Furthermore, the impact of human activities on the environment is becoming more and more apparent. The Earth's climate is warming, ecosystems are collapsing, and species are going extinct at an alarming rate.

One of the key challenges we face in embracing the urgency for pathways to a sustainable world is the inertia of our current systems. Many industries and governments are heavily invested in unsustainable practices, and changing these practices can be difficult and disruptive. However, the consequences of maintaining the status quo are far more severe. If we continue on our current trajectory, we may see widespread environmental degradation, increased social and economic inequality, and potential conflicts over scarce resources.

To address these challenges, we need to shift our mindset and embrace a more holistic and long-term approach to decision-making. This means considering the environmental, social, and economic impacts of our actions and seeking solutions that benefit all three pillars of sustainability. It also means recognizing that individual actions can make a difference and that we all have a role to play in creating a more sustainable world.

One of the key pathways to a sustainable world is transitioning to renewable sources of energy. Fossil fuels are a major contributor to greenhouse gas emissions and climate change. By investing in renewable energy technologies such as solar, wind, and geothermal power, we can reduce our carbon footprint and decrease our dependence on finite resources.

Another important pathway to sustainability is finding ways to minimize waste and promote circular economies. Currently, our linear economic model – where resources are extracted, used, and discarded – is unsustainable. By designing products with recyclability and reusability in mind, we can reduce waste and create closed-loop systems where materials are continually cycled back into the economy.

Additionally, we need to prioritize the conservation and restoration of ecosystems. Healthy ecosystems provide numerous benefits, including clean air and water, biodiversity, and climate regulation. Protecting and restoring natural habitats should be a priority to ensure the well-being of both humans and the planet.

Education and awareness are also crucial in embracing the urgency for pathways to a sustainable world. By promoting sustainable practices and values, we can empower individuals and communities to make informed choices and take action. Education should also focus on the interconnectedness of social and environmental issues, highlighting that sustainable development cannot be achieved without addressing social justice and equity.

In conclusion, embracing the urgency for pathways to a sustainable world is essential for the future of humanity and the planet. We must recognize the finite nature of our resources and the damaging effects of our actions on the environment. By shifting towards renewable energy, minimizing waste, conserving ecosystems, and promoting education and awareness, we can create a more sustainable and livable future for all. It will not be an easy task, but the potential rewards far outweigh the challenges. It is time to act now and embrace the urgency for a sustainable world.